TRUTH AND ACTU

J. Krishnamurti

TRUTH AND ACTUALITY

1817

HARPER & ROW, PUBLISHERS, San Francisco
Cambridge, Hagerstown, Philadelphia, New York,
London, Mexico City, São Paulo, Sydney

TRUTH AND ACTUALITY. Copyright © 1980 by Krishnamurti
Foundation Trust Ltd., London. All rights reserved. Printed in
the United States of America. No part of this book may be used
or reproduced in any manner whatsoever without written per-
mission except in the case of brief quotations embodied in critical
articles and reviews. For information address Harper & Row,
Publishers, Inc., 10 East 53rd Street, New York, NY 10022.
Published simultaneously in Canada by Fitzhenry & Whiteside,
Limited, Toronto.

Library of Congress Cataloging in Publication Data

Krishnamurti, Jiddu, 1895-
   Truth and actuality.

   Part 1 consists of discussions between J. Krishnamurti and
D. Bohm.
   1. Philosophy—Addresses, essays, lectures. I. Bohm, David.
II. Title.
B29.K74 1980   110   80-17545
ISBN 0-06-064875-9

---

80 81 82 83 84 10 9 8 7 6 5 4 3 2 1

Editor's Notes and Inscriptions

In Part I the discussions are taken from a series between J. Krishnamurti and David Bohm, professor of Theoretical Physics at London University. Part II is the Authentic Report of Talks and Dialogues at Brockwood Park which took place in the autumn of 1975. The Questions and Answers in Part II come from Talks at Saanen given in 1975 and 1976.

"What is the relationship between truth and reality? Reality being, as we said, all the things that thought has put together. Reality means, the root meaning of that word is, things or thing. And living in the world of things, which is reality, we want to establish a relationship with a world which has no things—which is impossible."

"Actuality means 'What is' . . . Are you facing in yourself what actually is going on . . You don't take actuality and look at it."

"Man has been concerned throughout the ages to discover or live in 'Truth'."

C. AND G. W D.

CONTENTS

Part I

*Discussions between J. Krishnamurti and
Professor David Bohm*

Chapter

1 REALITY, ACTUALITY, TRUTH   15
What is truth and what is reality? Is there any
connection? Reality as "res", "thing"—the
content of thought and consciousness.
Reality independent of thought: nature. Illusion,
the false, as part of reality.
Actuality, the fact. Every thing conditioned and
determining every other thing: all inter-related.
Thought is part of this. Reality as experienced
cannot be independent of man.
Consciousness as reality can run straight or
crookedly.
The sane, whole man's thread runs straight. The
sane, whole man *is* truth.
Truth includes all that is, it is one. Reality is
multiple, conditioned. The true man comprehends
reality and its conditioning.
What is the relation of the scholar's knowledge of
reality to truth? Can human consciousness, which
is adulterated and runs false, comprehend truth?
The false mirror of consciousness.
Reality creates its own energy. What is the energy
of truth? Truth comprehends reality (not *vice*

versa): then reality runs true. Meditation is not
moving from one reality to another.

2   INSIGHT AND TRUTH. GULF BETWEEN REALITY AND
    TRUTH   27
Insight—action not of thought but of truth.
Attempt to convey insight means a time-process.
The action of reasoned thought is different from
insight. Is there a thinking which is non-verbal?
Has thought through which insight works a
different order from other thought?
How does insight take place? There must be
insight before thought realises its limitations.
The energy and force of insight; the weight of
habit and conditioning.
Thought can't dissolve conditioning. What will?
Example: insight into "the observer is the
observed" (the thinker is the thought).
Truth is different from reality but men are tied to
reality. Is the energy of truth different from that
of reality? The gulf between reality and truth.
"You come along with a basketful and I do not
know how to receive it."
No path to truth in the field of reality. The drum
vibrates because it is empty. Reality is everything; truth is no-thingness.
The mind must be an empty house. What is the
action of that emptiness in my life?
We need truth and actuality, but our minds are
occupied with reality. We seek security in reality;
in nothingness there is complete security. Psychological and physical security discussed. A mind
rooted in nothingness operates in the field of reality
with intelligence.

To depend for security on the world of reality brings about inward disorganisation.

3 THE SEED OF TRUTH   44
The seed. A mystery which thought cannot touch; it is beyond the field of reality.
Limitless progress is possible in the field of reality, but the essence escapes. The truth of that mystery empties the mind. Order in reality brings a certain silence to the mind, but this is not the total silence in which the truth of that mystery *is*.

Part II

Talks and Dialogues

4 RIGHT ACTION   55
What is right action in this disintegrating world? The word "religious". The fragmentary nature of thought. Freedom "from all the things thought has created in us". The tricks of thought. "You cannot go through reality to come to truth." Thought and the content of consciousness. Can there be order in the world of reality? To be aware of disorder. Reality and truth. About asking questions.
Questions: (1) Order and disorder; total perception. (2) Observation without the division caused by the "me". (3) Must we always live in crisis and challenge? (4) "Facing a terrible void"; has life significance? (5) Thought is afraid not to think.

5 THE PROBLEM OF FEAR   72
Can one be free of fear? Energy; the energy of duality; thought as a process of friction. Is there

another kind of energy. Desire and its arising.
Why is there the inward sense of lack or want?
Trying to fill the void; the movement of desire as
thought, time and measure.
Failure to face "what is". Does desire create fear?
The root of fear. Psychological time; is it a projection of thought? Thought as becoming in
psychological time. Fragmentary divisions of
thought.
To observe but not to analyse. Observing fear
without naming, rationalising. Pursuit of desire
and pleasure. Suffering and the consciousness of
man. "We love God and kill human beings."
Suffering; to "remain solidly with it".
Another energy.

6 DIALOGUE—I   86
Questions about the biography ("The Years of
Awakening"). The idea of the Bodhisattva or
Avatar; the unconditioned mind.
Awareness. The question of choice. Awareness as
total sensitivity. Awareness is choiceless. Attention and responding from a centre. "Is there an
activity which is not mechanical?" Functioning
from conditioning and from past experience.
Thought is mechanical. Is there a part of the mind
untouched by conditioning? The mechanical must
be understood first. Hurts; being hurt and past
hurts.
Image-forming. Clinging to the known, the image.
Seeking security in words and images. Awareness
without the observer. Security and being nothing.

7 DIALOGUE—II   107
Questions: (1) "I cannot see the whole of the
observer because I only see in fragments." (2)

"Attention requires tremendous vitality that we don't have." Observation must begin in relationship. To be related means to respond accurately; accuracy means with care. But one is related through images built by thought; inaccurate response. Are we aware of the images? Are images necessary? "Is life a process of infinite conflicts?" Chaos caused by images. Attention, inattention and image-forming. Relationship between one with images, another without. Changing one image for another (gurus). Can thought dispel images? Burdened with the past. First step: be aware you have images. "Learn about yourself, actually as you are." "Don't look from the past." No authority. "Psychologically the guru is 'me'." Lack of attention and paying attention to inattention.

8 SUFFERING; THE MEANING OF DEATH   130
Three active principles: fear, pleasure, suffering. Physical and psychological suffering. Suffering distorts and darkens. Factors of suffering; attachment to ideas, persons, to the past. To remain totally with suffering. Looking at suffering without the observer. Compassion gives a different kind of energy. The creative mind. The consciousness of the world. Death. Can time have a stop? Psychological time. The "me" is the essence of time. Re-incarnation; resurrection. Immortality, eternity. What happens at death with the "me" and "not me" unresolved? The stream of human consciousness—the movement of time in which all human beings are caught. The mutation in consciousness.

Questions: (1) To transform consciousness: is this an ideal? (2) The Christian message and your message: there is no message.

9   THE SACRED, RELIGION, MEDITATION   144
Truth and its world of reality. Religion as a gathering together of energy. Reality is the world of things built on thought which is material and mechanical. Truth has no place there. Need to bring about order in the world of reality. Thought has created disorder; how will order come about? The observation of disorder without thought. Can thought as time and measure come to a stop? Freedom and authority. The art of pure listening, seeing, learning. Control, comparison and attention: is a mutation possible? "There is no ending in the world of reality of time." Stillness and the timeless. Significance of meditation.

Part III
Some Questions and Answers

10   RIGHT LIVELIHOOD   159

11   WILL   161

12   EMOTIONS AND THOUGHT   163

13   BEAUTY   164

14   THE STREAM OF "SELFISHNESS"   166

15   THE UNIFYING FACTOR   170

PART I

Discussions between J. Krishnamurti and Professor David Bohm

Chapter 1

REALITY, ACTUALITY, TRUTH

KRISHNAMURTI : I was thinking about the question of what is truth and what is reality and whether there is any relationship between the two, or whether they are separate. Are they eternally divorced, or are they just projections of thought? And if thought didn't operate, would there be reality? I thought that reality comes from "res", thing, and that anything that thought operates on, or fabricates, or reflects about, is reality. And thought, thinking in a distorted, conditioned manner is illusion, is self-deception, is distortion. I left it there, because I wanted to let it come rather than my pursuing it.

Dr Bohm: The question of thought and reality and truth has occupied philosophers over the ages. It's a very difficult one. It seems to me that what you say is basically true, but there are a lot of points that need to be ironed out. One of the questions that arises is this : if reality is thought, what thought thinks about, what appears in consciousness, does it go beyond consciousness?

K : Are the contents of consciousness reality?

Dr B: That's the question; and can we use thought as equivalent to consciousness in its basic form?

K : Yes.

Dr B: I wonder whether, just for the sake of completeness, we should include in thought also feeling, desire, will and reaction.

I feel we should, if we are exploring the connection between consciousness, reality and truth.

K : Yes.

Dr B: One of the points I'd like to bring up is : there is thought, there is our consciousness, and there is the thing of which we are conscious. And as you have often said, the thought is not the thing.

K : Yes.

Dr B: We have to get it clear, because in some sense the thing may have some kind of reality independent of thought; we can't go so far as to deny all that. Or do we go as far as some philosophers, like Bishop Berkeley, who has said that all is thought? Now I would like to suggest a possibly useful distinction between that reality which is largely created by our own thought, or by the thought of mankind, and that reality which one can regard as existing independently of this thought. For example, would you say Nature is real?

K : It is, yes.

Dr B: And it is not just our own thoughts.

K : No, obviously not.

Dr B: The tree, the whole earth, the stars.

K : Of course, the cosmos. Pain is real.

Dr B: Yes. I was thinking the other day, illusion is real, in the sense that it is really something going on, to a person who is in a state of illusion.

K : To him it is real.

Dr B: But to us it is also real because his brain is in a certain state of electrical and chemical movement, and he acts from his illusion in a real way.

K: In a real way, in a distorted way.

Dr B: Distorted but real. Now it occurred to me that one could say that even the false is real but not true. This might be important.

K: I understand. For instance : is Christ real?

Dr B: He is certainly real in the minds of people who believe in Him, in the sense we have been discussing.

K: We want to find out the distinction between truth and reality. We said anything that thought thinks about, whether unreasonably or reasonably, is a reality. It may be distorted or reasoned clearly, it is still a reality. That reality, I say, has nothing to do with truth.

Dr B: Yes, but we have to say besides, that in some way reality involves more than mere thought. There is also the question of actuality. Is the thing actual? Is its existence an actual fact? According to the dictionary, the fact means what is actually done, what actually happens, what is actually perceived.

K: Yes, we must understand what we mean by the fact.

Dr B: The fact is the action that is actually taking place. Suppose, for example, that you are walking on a dark road and that you think you see something. It may be real, it may not be real. One moment you feel that it's real and the next moment that it's not real. But then you suddenly touch it and it resists your movement. From this action it's immediately clear that there is a real thing which you have contacted. But if there is no such contact you say that it's not real, that it was perhaps an illusion, or at least something mistakenly taken as real.

K: But, of course, that thing is still a reality that thought thinks about. And reality has nothing to do with truth.

Dr B: But now, let us go further with the discussion of "the

thing". You see, the root of the English word "thing" is fundamentally the same as the German "bedingen", to condition,
to set the conditions or determine. And indeed we must agree
that a thing is necessarily conditioned.

K : It is conditioned. Let's accept that.

Dr B: This is a key point. Any form of reality is conditioned.
Thus, an illusion is still a form of reality which is conditioned.
For example, the man's blood may have a different constitu-
tion because he's not in a balanced state. He is distorting, he
may be too excited, and that could be why he is caught in
illusion. So every thing is determined by conditions and it also
conditions every other thing.

K : Yes, quite.

Dr B: All things are inter-related in the way of mutual conditioning which we call influence. In physics that's very clear,
the planets all influence each other, the atoms influence each
other, and I wanted to suggest that maybe we could regard
thought and consciousness as part of this whole chain of
influence.

K : Quite right.

Dr B: So that every thing can influence consciousness and it in
turn can work back and influence the shapes of things, as we
make objects. And you could then say that this is all reality,
that thought is therefore also real.

K : Thought is real.

Dr B: And there is one part of reality influencing another part
of reality.

K : Also, one part of illusion influences another part of illusion.

Dr B: Yes, but now we have to be careful because we can say
there is that reality which is not made by man, by mankind.

But that's still limited. The cosmos, for example, as seen by us is influenced by our own experience and therefore limited.

K: Quite.

Dr B: Any thing that we see, we see through our own experience, our own background. So that reality cannot possibly be totally independent of man.

K: No.

Dr B: It may be relatively independent. The tree is a reality that is relatively independent but it's our consciousness that abstracts the tree.

K: Are you saying that man's reality is the product of influence and conditioning?

Dr B: Yes, mutual interaction and reaction.

K: And all his illusions are also his product.

Dr B: Yes, they are all mixed together.

K: And what is the relationship of a sane, rational, healthy, whole man, to reality and to truth?

Dr B: Yes, we must consider that, but first may we look at this question of truth. I think the derivation of words is often very useful. The word "true" in Latin, which is "verus", means "that which is". The same as the English "was" and "were", or German "wahr". Now in English the root meaning of the word "true" is honest and faithful; you see, we can often say that a line is true, or a machine is true. There was a story I once read about a thread that ran so true; it was using the image of a spinning-wheel with the thread running straight.

K: Quite.

Dr B: And now we can say that our thought, or our consciousness, is true to that which is, if it is running straight, if the man is sane and healthy. And otherwise it is not, it is false. So the falseness of consciousness is not just wrong information, but it is actually running crookedly as a reality.

K : So you're saying, as long as man is sane, healthy, whole and rational, his thread is always straight.

Dr B: Yes, his consciousness is on a straight thread. Therefore his reality—

K : —is different from the reality of a man whose thread is crooked, who is irrational, who is neurotic.

Dr B: Very different. Perhaps the latter is even insane. You can see with insane people how different it is—they sometimes cannot even see the same reality at all.

K : And the sane, healthy, whole, holy man, what is his relationship to truth?

Dr B: If you accept the meaning of the word, if you say truth is that which is, as well as being true to that which is, then you have to say that he is all this.

K : So you would say the man who is sane, whole, is truth?

Dr B: He is truth, yes.

K : Such a man is truth. He may think certain things which would be reality, but he is truth. He can't think irrationally.

Dr B: Well, I wouldn't say quite that, I'd say that he can make a mistake.

K : Of course.

Dr B: But he doesn't persist in it. In other words, there is the man who has made a mistake and acknowledges it, changes it.

K : Yes, quite right.

Dr B: And there is also the man who has made a mistake but his mind is not straight and therefore he goes on with it. But we have to come back to the question : does truth go beyond any particular man; does it include other men, and Nature as well?

K : It includes all that is.

Dr B: Yes, so the truth is one. But there are many different things in the field of reality. Each thing is conditioned, the whole field of reality is conditioned. But clearly, truth itself cannot be conditioned or dependent on things.

K : What then is the relationship to reality of the man who is truth?

Dr B: He sees all the things and, in doing this, he comprehends reality. What the word "comprehends" means is to hold it all together.

K : He doesn't separate reality. He says, "I comprehend it, I hold it, I see it".

Dr B: Yes, it's all one field of reality, himself and everything. But it has things in it which are conditioned and he comprehends the conditions.

K : And because he comprehends conditioning, he is free of conditioning.

Dr B: It seems clear then that all our knowledge, being based on thought, is actually a part of this one conditioned field of reality.

K : Now another question. Suppose I am a scholar, I'm full of such conditioned and conditioning knowledge. How am I to comprehend truth in the sense of holding it all together?

Dr B: I don't think you can comprehend truth.

K : Say I have studied all my life, I've devoted all my life to knowledge, which is reality.

Dr B: Yes, and it is also about a bigger reality.

K : And suppose you come along and say, "Truth is some-where else, it's not that". I accept you, because you show it to me, and so I say, "Please help me to move from here to that".

Dr B: Yes.

K : Because once I get that, I comprehend it. If I live here, then my comprehension is always fragmented.

Dr B: Yes.

K : Therefore my knowledge tells me, "This is reality but it is not truth". And suppose you come along and say, "No, it is not". And I ask : please tell me how to move from here to that.

Dr B: Well, we've just said we can't move . . .

K : I'm putting it briefly. What am I to do?

Dr B: I think I have to see that this whole structure of know-ledge is inevitably false, because my reality is twisted.

K : Would you say the content of my consciousness is knowledge?

Dr B: Yes.

K : How am I to empty that consciousness and yet retain knowledge which is not twisted—otherwise I can't function—and reach a state, or whatever it is, which will comprehend reality. I don't know if I'm making myself clear.

Dr B: Yes.

K : What I'm asking is : my human consciousness *is* its content, which is knowledge; it's a messy conglomeration of irrational knowledge and some which is correct. Can that consciousness comprehend, or bring into itself, truth?

Dr B: No, it can't.

K : Therefore, can this consciousness go to that truth? It can't either. Then what?

Dr B: There can be a perception of the falseness in this consciousness. This consciousness is false, in the sense that it does not run true. Because of the confused content it does not run true.

K : It's contradictory.

Dr B: It muddles things up.

K : Not, "muddles things up"; it *is* a muddle.

Dr B: It is a muddle, yes, in the way it moves. Now then, one of the main points of the muddle is that when consciousness reflects on itself, the reflection has this character : it's as if there were a mirror and consciousness were looking at itself through a mirror and the mirror is reflecting consciousness as if it were not consciousness but an independent reality.

K : Yes.

Dr B: Now therefore, the action which consciousness takes is wrong, because it tries to improve the apparently independent reality, whereas in fact to do this is just a muddle.

I would like to put it this way : the whole of consciousness is somehow an instrument which is connected up to a deeper energy. And as long as consciousness is connected in that way, it maintains its state of wrong action.

K : Yes.

Dr B: So on seeing that this consciousnes is reflecting itself wrongly as independent of thought, what is needed is somehow to disconnect the energy of consciousness. The whole of consciousness has to be disconnected, so it would, as it were, lie there without energy.

K : You're saying, don't feed it. My consciousness is a muddle, it is confused, contradictory, and all the rest of it. And its very contradiction, its very muddle, gives its own energy.

Dr B: Well, I would say that the energy is not actually coming from consciousness, but that as long as the energy is coming, consciousness keeps the muddle going.

K : From where does it come?

Dr B: We'd have to say that perhaps it comes from something deeper.

K : If it comes from something deeper, then we enter into the whole field of gods and outside agency and so on.

Dr B: No, I wouldn't say the energy comes from an outside agency. I would prefer to say it comes from me, in some sense.

K : Then the "me" is this consciousness?

Dr B: Yes.

K : So the content is creating its own energy. Would you say that?

Dr B: In some sense it is. But the puzzle is that it seems impossible for this content to create its own energy. That would be saying that the content is able to create its own energy.

K : Actually, the content *is* creating its own energy. Look, I'm in contradiction and that very contradiction gives me vitality. I have got opposing desires. When I have opposing desires I have energy, I fight. Therefore that desire is creating the energy—not God, or something profounder—it is still desire. This is the trick that so many played. They say there is an outside agency, a deeper energy—but then one's back in the old field. But I realise the energy of contradiction, the energy of desire, of will, of pursuit, of pleasure, all that which is the content of my consciousness—which *is* consciousness—is creating its own energy. Reality is this; reality is creating its own energy. I may say, "I derive my energy deep down", but it's still reality.

Dr B: Yes, suppose we accept that, but the point is that seeing the truth of this . . .

K : . . . that's what I want to get at. Is this energy different from the energy of truth?

Dr B: Yes.

K : It is different.

Dr B: But let's try to put it like this : reality may have many levels of energy.

K : Yes.

Dr B: But a certain part of the energy has gone off the straight line. Let's say the brain feeds energy to all the thought processes. Now, if somehow the brain didn't feed energy to the thought process that is confused, then the thing might straighten out.

K : That's it. If this energy runs along the straight thread it is a reality without contradiction. It's an energy which is endless because it has no friction. Now is that energy different from the energy of truth?

Dr B: Yes. They are different, and as we once discussed, there must be a deeper common source.

K : I'm not sure. You are suggesting that they both spring out of the same root.

Dr B: That's what I suggest. But for the moment there is the energy of truth which can comprehend the reality and—

K : —the other way it cannot.

Dr B: No, it cannot; but there appears to be some connection in the sense that when truth comprehends reality, reality goes straight. So there appears to be a connection at least one way.

K : That's right, a one-way connection—truth loves this, this doesn't love truth.

Dr B: But once the connection has been made, then reality runs true and does not waste energy or make confusion.

K : You see, that's where meditation comes in. Generally, meditation is from here to there, with practice and all the rest of it. To move from this to that.

Dr B: Move from one reality to another.

K : That's right. Meditation is actually seeing what is. But generally meditation is taken as moving from one reality to another.

Chapter 2

INSIGHT AND TRUTH. GULF
BETWEEN REALITY AND TRUTH

KRISHNAMURTI: I am concerned with trying to find out if there is an action which is not a process of thought, an action which is of truth—if I can put it that way—an insight which acts instantly. I want to inquire into that question.

Dr Bohm: Perhaps one action that acts instantly is to see falseness.

K : Yes. It's difficult to take examples. I have an insight into the fact that people believe in God—I'm taking that as an example.

Dr B: What is the nature of your insight, then?

K : The insight into the fact that God is their projection.

Dr B: Yes, and therefore false.

K : I have an insight. If I had a belief in God it would drop instantly. So it is not a process of thought, it is an insight into truth.

Dr B: Or into falseness.

K : Or into falseness, and that action is complete, it's over and done with. I don't know if I'm conveying it : that action is whole, there is no regret, there is no personal advantage, there is no emotion. It is an action which is complete. Whereas the action brought about by thought, the investigation of an analysis whether there is a God or no God, is always incomplete.

Dr B: Yes, I understand that. Then there is another action, in which you do use words, where you try to realise the insight. Let's say, you talk to people. Is that action complete or incomplete? Say you have discovered about God. Other people are still calling this a fact, and therefore ...

K : But the man speaks from an insight.

Dr B: He speaks from an insight, but at the same time he starts a process of time.

K : Yes, to convey something.

Dr B: To change things. Let's now consider that just to get it clear. It's starting from an insight but it's conveying truth.

K : Yes, but it's always starting from an insight.

Dr B: And in doing that you may have to organise ...

K : ... reasonable thinking and so on, of course. And the action of reasoned thought is different from the action of insight.

Dr B: Now what is the difference when insight is conveyed through reasoned thought? To come back again to your insight about God : you have to convey it to other people, you must put it into a reasonable form.

K : Yes.

Dr B: And therefore isn't there still some of the quality of the insight, as you convey it? You must find a reasonable way to convey it. Therefore in doing that, some of the truth of the insight is still being communicated in this form. And in some sense that is thought.

K : No, when conveying to another that insight verbally, one's action will be incomplete unless *he* has insight.

Dr B: That's right. So you must convey what will give someone an insight.

K : Can you give an insight?

Dr B: Not really, but whatever you convey must somehow do something which perhaps cannot be further described.

K : Yes. That can only happen when you yourself have dropped the belief in God.

Dr B: But there is no guarantee that it will happen.

K : No, of course not.

Dr B: That depends on the other person, whether he is ready to listen.

K : So we come to this point : is there a thinking which is non-verbal? Would this be what communicates insight?

Dr B: I would say there is a kind of thinking that communicates insight. The insight is non-verbal, but the thinking itself is not non-verbal. There is the kind of thinking which is dominated by the word and there is another kind of thinking whose order is determined, not by the word, but by the insight.

K : Is the insight the product of thought?

Dr B: No, but insight works through thought. Insight is never the product of thought.

K : Obviously not.

Dr B: But it may work through thought. I wanted to say that the thought through which insight is working has a different order from the other kind of thought. I want to distinguish those two. You once gave an example of a drum vibrating from the emptiness within. I took it to mean that the action of the skin was like the action of thought. Is that right?

K : Yes, that's right. Now, how does insight take place? Because if it is not the product of thought, not the process of organised thought and all the rest of it, then how does this insight come into being?

Dr B: It's not clear what you mean by the question.

K : How do I have an insight that God is a projection of our own desires, images and so on? I see the falseness of it or the truth of it; how does it take place?

Dr B: I don't see how you could expect to describe it.

K : I have a feeling inside that thought cannot possibly enter into an area where insight, where truth is, although it operates anywhere else. But truth, that area, can operate through thought.

Dr B: Yes.

K : But thought cannot enter into that area.

Dr B: That seems clear. We say that thought is the response of memory. It seems clear that this cannot be unconditioned and free.

K : I would like to go into this question, if I may : how does insight take place? If it is not the process of thought, then what is the quality of the mind, or the quality of observation, in which thought doesn't enter? And because it doesn't enter, you have an insight. We said, insight is complete. It is not fragmented as thought is. So thought cannot bring about an insight.

Dr B: Thought may communicate the insight. Or it may communicate some of the data which lead you to an insight. For example, people told you about religion and so on, but eventually the insight depends on something which is not thought.

K: Then how does that insight come? Is it a cessation of thought?

Dr B: It could be considered as a cessation.

K: Thought itself realises that it cannot enter into a certain area. That is, the thinker is the thought, the observer, the experiencer, all the rest of it; and thought itself realises, becomes aware, that it can only function within a certain area.

Dr B: Doesn't that itself require insight? Before thought realises that, there must be an insight.

K: That's just it. Does thought realise that there must be insight?

Dr B: I don't know, but I'm saying there would have to be insight into the nature of thought before thought would realise anything. Because it seems to me that thought by itself cannot realise anything of this kind.

K: Yes.

Dr B: But in some way, we said, truth can operate in thought, in reality.

K: Truth can operate in the field of reality. Now how does one's mind see the truth? Is it a process?

Dr B: You're asking whether there is a process of seeing. There is no process, that would be time.

K: That's right.

Dr B: Let's consider a certain point, that there is an insight about the nature of thought, that the observer is the observed and so on.

31

K : That's clear.

Dr B: Now in some sense thought must accept that insight, carry it, respond to it.

K : Or the insight is so vital, so energetic, so full of vitality, that it forces thought to operate.

Dr B: All right, then there is the necessity to operate.

K : Yes, the necessity.

Dr B: But you see, generally speaking it doesn't have that vitality. So in some indirect way thought has rejected the insight, at least it appears to be so.

K : Most people have an insight, but habit is so strong they reject it.

Dr B: I'm trying to get to the bottom of it, to see if we can break through that rejection.

K : Break through the rejection, break through the habit, the conditioning, which prevents the insight. Though one may have an insight, the conditioning is so strong, you reject the insight. This is what happens.

Dr B: I looked up the word "habit" and it says, "A settled disposition of the mind", which seems very good. The mind is disposed in a certain fixed way which resists change. Now we get caught in the same question : how are we going to break that "very settled disposition"?

K : I don't think you can break it, I don't think thought can break it.

Dr B: We are asking for that intense insight which necessarily dissolves it.

K : So, to summarise : one has an insight into truth and reality.

One's mind is disposed in a certain way, it has formed habits in the world of reality—it *lives* there.

Dr B: It's very rigid.

K : Now suppose you come along and point out the rigidity of it. I catch a glimpse of what you're saying—which is non-thinking—and I see it.

Dr B: In a glimpse only.

K : In a glimpse. But this conditioning is so strong I reject it.

Dr B: I don't do it purposely; it just happens.

K : It has happened because you helped to create that happening. Is that glimpse, first of all, strong enough to dissolve this? If it is not so strong, then it goes on. Can this conditioning dissolve? You see, I must have an insight into the conditioning, otherwise I can't dissolve it.

Dr B: Maybe we could look at it like this : conditioning is a reality, a very solid reality, which is fundamentally what we think about.

K : Yes.

Dr B: As we said in the previous dialogue, it's actual. Ordinary reality is not only what I think about, but it fits actuality to some extent—the actual fact. That's the proof of its reality. Now, at first sight it seems that this conditioning is just as solid as any reality, if not more solid.

K : Much more solid. Is that conditioning dissolved, does it come to an end through thinking?

Dr B: It won't because thinking is what it is.

K : So thinking won't dissolve it. Then what will?

Dr B: We're back again. We see that it's only truth, insight.

K : I think something takes place. I see I'm conditioned and I separate myself from the conditioning, I am different from the conditioning. And you come along and say "No, it isn't like that, the observer is the observed". If I can see, or have an insight, that the observer is the observed, then the conditioning begins to dissolve.

Dr B: Because it's not solid.

K : The perception of that is the ending of the conditioning. The truth is, when there is the realisation that the observer is the observed. Then in that realisation, which is truth, the conditioning disappears. How does it disappear? What is necessary for the crumbling of that structure?

Dr B: The insight into the falseness of it.

K : But I can have an insight into something that is false and yet I go on that way, accept the false and live in the false.

Dr B: Yes.

K : Now I don't know if I can convey something. I want to bring this into action in my life. I have accepted reality as truth, I live in that—my gods, my habits, everything—I live in that. You come along and say "Look, truth is different from reality" and you explain it to me. How will I put away that tremendous weight, or break that tremendous conditioning? I need energy to break that conditioning. Does the energy come when I see, "the observer is the observed"? As we've said, I see the importance, rationally, that the conditioning must break down, I see the necessity of it : I see how it operates, the division, the conflict and all the rest of what is involved. Now when I realise that the observer is the observed, a totally different kind of energy comes into being. That's all I want to get at.

Dr B: Yes, it's not the energy of reality then. I see it better when I say, "the thinker is the thought". It's actually the same thing.

K : Yes, the thinker is the thought. Now, is that energy different from the energy of conditioning and the activity of the conditioning and reality? Is that energy the perception of truth?—and therefore it has quite a different quality of energy.

Dr B: It seems to have the quality of being free of, not being bound by the conditioning.

K : Yes. Now I want to make it practical to myself. I see this whole thing that you have described to me. I have got a fairly good mind, I can argue, explain it, all the rest of it, but this quality of energy doesn't come. And you want me to have this quality, out of your compassion, out of your understanding, out of your perception of truth. You say, "Please, see that". And I can't see it, because I'm always living in the realm of reality. You are living in the realm of truth and I can't. There is no relationship between you and me. I accept your word, I see the reason for it, I see the logic of it, I see the actuality of it, but I can't break it down.

How will you help—I'm using that word hesitantly—how can you help me to break this down? It's your job, because you see the truth and I don't. You say, "For God's sake, see this". How will you help me? Through words? Then we enter into the realm with which I am quite familiar. This is actually going on, you understand? So what is one to do? What will you do with me, who refuses to see something which is just there? And you point out that as long as we live in this world of reality, there is going to be murder, death—everything that goes on there. There is no answer in that realm for any of our problems. How will you convey this to me? I want to find out, I'm very keen, I want to get out of this.

Dr B: It's only possible to communicate the intensity. We already discussed all the other factors that are communicated.

K : You see, what you say has no system, no method, because they are all part of the conditioning. You say something totally new, unexpected, to which I haven't even given a single moment of thought. You come along with a basketful and I do not know how to receive you. This has been really a problem; to the prophets, to every . . .

Dr B: It seems nobody has really succeeded in it.

K : Nobody has. It's part of education that keeps us constantly in the realm of reality.

Dr B: Everyone is expecting a path marked out in the field of reality.

K : You talk of a totally different kind of energy from the energy of reality. And you say that energy will wipe all this out, but it will use this reality.

Dr B: Yes, it will work through it.

K : It's all words to me, because society, education, economics, my parents, everything is here in reality. All the scientists are working here, all the professors, all the economists, everybody is here. And you say "Look", and I refuse to look.

Dr B: It's not even that one refuses, it's something more unconscious perhaps.

K : So in discussing this, is there a thinking which is not in the realm of reality?

Dr B: One might ask whether there is such thought, in the sense of the response of the drum to the emptiness within.

K : That's a good simile. Because it is empty, it is vibrating.

Dr B: The material thing is vibrating to the emptiness.

K : The material thing is vibrating. Wait—is truth nothingness?

36

Dr B: Reality is some *thing*, perhaps every *thing*. Truth is no *thing*. That is what the word "nothing" deeply means. So truth is "no-thingness".

K : Yes, truth is nothing.

Dr B: Because if it's not reality it must be nothing—no thing.

K : And therefore empty. Empty being—how did you once describe it?

Dr B: Leisure is the word—leisure means basically "empty". The English root of "empty" means at leisure, unoccupied.

K : So you are saying to me, "Your mind must be unoccupied". It mustn't be occupied by reality.

Dr B: Yes, that's clear.

K : So it must be empty, there mustn't be a thing in it which has been put together by reality, by thought—no thing. Nothing means that.

Dr B: It's clear that things are what we think about, therefore we have to say the mind must not think about anything.

K : That's right. That means thought cannot think about emptiness.

Dr B: That would make it into a thing.

K : That's just it. You see, Hindu tradition says you can come to it.

Dr B: Yes, but anything you come to must be by a path which is marked out in the field of reality.

K : Yes. Now, I have an insight into that, I see it. I see my mind must be unoccupied, must have no inhabitants, must be an empty house. What is the action of that emptiness in my life?—because I must live here; I don't know why, but I must live here. I want to find out, is that action different from the other action? It must be, and therefore . . .

Dr B: It has to be.

K: And how am I to empty my mind of the content which makes up consciousness? How am I to empty the content? Content is reality, my consciousness is reality.

Dr B: Yes, the consciousness is reality. It's not merely consciousness of reality.

K: No, consciousness *is* reality. And how is that content to be emptied, so that it is not reality—let's put it that way.

Dr B: Yes, so it would be no thing.

K: How is it to be done?

Dr B: We've often gone into this question of "how" already. There's something wrong with the question.

K: Of course, something is wrong, because the very word "how" means reality, thought and all the rest of it. Do a miracle!

Dr B: That's what we need.

K: How can you bring about a miracle in a man who lives in this consciousness with its content? I'm trying to find out, is there any action which will dissolve the whole content? Consciousness is not of reality, consciousness *is* reality. That, I think, is the difference.

Dr B: Let's try to make it more clear. Consciousness is ordinarily thought to reflect reality. But it *is* reality. In some way we should make it clear that consciousness reflects on what is actual. For example, we have the reality of the table in our minds and we may see its actual effect. So that consciousness is some peculiar combination of reality and actuality, so far as I can see.

K : Yes, I accept that.

Dr B: Could I put it that instead we need truth and actuality. Could I say that the emptiness works in actuality from truth, that the act of emptiness is actuality too.

K : Yes. But we are not in the state of the working of emptiness in actuality. One's mind is always occupied with desires, problems, sex, money, God, what people say—it's never empty.

Dr B: When we start from where we are, it will not be much use to discuss how the empty mind will act because, as you said, our mind is now occupied.

K : You see, after all, one is seeking complete security, that's what one wants, and one is seeking security in reality. Therefore one rejects any other security.

Dr B: Yes, I think there is a conviction that reality is all there is, and that this is the only place where you could find it.

K : Yes. And suppose you come along and say, "Look, in nothingness there is complete security".

Dr B: Yes, let's discuss that, because at first sight it may seem very implausible.

K : Of course.

Dr B: One might ask how anything can come out of nothing.

K : Just a minute. I say to you, "In nothingness there is complete security and stability". You listen and you get an insight into it because you're attentive and there is a conversation going on between us. And you say, "That is so". But your mind, which is occupied, says, "What on earth does this mean? It's nonsense."

Dr B: Perhaps that would be the first reaction. But later it would be more like this : it sounds reasonable on one side, but

39

on the other side you do have to take care of your real material needs.

K : That's understood.

Dr B: There arises a conflict because what you are proposing appears to be reasonable, but it doesn't seem to take care of your material needs. Without having taken care of these needs you're not secure.

K : Therefore they call the world of reality "maya".

Dr B: Why is that? How do you make the connection?

K : Because they say, to live in emptiness is necessary and if you live there you consider the world as maya.

Dr B: You could say all that stuff is illusion, but then you would find you were in real danger . . .

K : Of course.

Dr B: So you seem to be calling for a confidence that nothingness will take care of you, physically and in every way. In other words, from nothingness, you say, there is security.

K : No, *in* nothingness there is security.

Dr B: And this security must include physical security.

K : No, I say, psychological security . . .

Dr B: Yes, but the question almost immediately arises . . .

K : How am I to be secure in the world of reality?

Dr B: Yes, because one could say : I accept that it will remove my psychological problems, but I still have to be physically secure as well in the world of reality.

K : There is no psychological security in reality, but only complete security in nothingness. Then if that is so, to me, my whole activity in the world of reality is entirely different.

Dr B: I see that, but the question will always be raised: is it different enough to ...

K: Oh yes, it would be totally different, because I'm not nationalistic, I'm not "English", I am nothing. Therefore our whole world is different. I don't divide ...

Dr B: Let's bring back your example of one who understands and the one who wants to communicate to the other. Somehow what doesn't communicate is the assurance that it will take care of all that.

K: It won't take care of all that. I have to *work* here.

Dr B: Well, according to what you said, there is a certain implication that in nothingness we will be completely secure in every way.

K: That is so, absolutely.

Dr B: Yes, but we have to ask: what about the physical security?

K: Physical security in reality? At present there is no security. I am fighting all my life, battling economically, socially, religiously. If I am inwardly, psychologically, completely secure, then my activity in the world of reality is born of complete intelligence. This doesn't exist now, because that intelligence is the perception of the whole and so on. As long as I'm "English" or "something", I cannot have security. I must work to get rid of that.

Dr B: I can see you'd become more intelligent, you'd become more secure—of course. But when you say "complete security" there is always the question: is it complete?

K: Oh, it is complete, psychologically.

Dr B: But not necessarily physically.

K : That feeling of complete security, inwardly, makes me ...

Dr B: It makes you do the right thing.

K : The right thing in the world of reality.

Dr B: Yes, I see that. You can be as secure as you can possibly be if you are completely intelligent, but you cannot guarantee that nothing is going to happen to you.

K : No, of course not. My mind is rooted, or established, in nothingness, and it operates in the field of reality with intelligence. That intelligence says, "There you cannot have security unless you do these things".

Dr B: I've got to do everything right.

K : Everything right according to that intelligence, which is of truth, of nothingness.

Dr B: And yet, if something does happen to you, nevertheless you still are secure.

K : Of course—if my house burns down. But you see we are seeking security here, in the world of reality.

Dr B: Yes, I understand that.

K : Therefore there is no security.

Dr B: As long as one feels that the world of reality is all there is, you have to seek it there.

K : Yes.

Dr B: One can see that in the world of reality there is in fact no security. Everything depends on other things which are unknown, and so on. That's why there is this intense fear.

K : You mention fear. In nothingness there is complete security, therefore no fear. But that sense of no fear has a totally different kind of activity in the world of reality. I have no fear—I work. I won't be rich or poor—I work. I work, not as an Englishman, a German, an Arab—all the rest of that nonsense—I work there intelligently. Therefore I am creating security in the world of reality. You follow?

Dr B: Yes, you're making it as secure as it can possibly be. The more clear and intelligent you are, the more secure it is.

K : Because inwardly I'm secure, I create security outwardly.

Dr B: On the other hand, if I feel that I depend inwardly on the world of reality, then I become disorganised inwardly.

K : Of course.

Dr B: Everybody does feel that he depends inwardly on the world of reality.

K : So the next thing is : you tell me this and I don't see it. I don't see the extraordinary beauty, the feeling, the depth of what you are saying about complete inward security. Therefore I say, "Look, how are you going to give the beauty of that to me?"

Chapter 3

THE SEED OF TRUTH

KRISHNAMURTI: If a seed of truth is planted it must operate, it must grow, it must function, it has a life of its own.

Dr Bohm: Many millions of people may have read or heard what you say. It may seem that a large number of them haven't understood. Do you feel that they are all going eventually to see it?

K: No, but it's going on, they are worried about it, they ask, "What does he mean by this?" The seed is functioning, it's growing, it isn't dead. You can say something false and that also operates.

Dr B: Yes, but now we have a struggle between those two and we cannot foresee the outcome of this struggle; we can't be sure of the outcome.

K: You plant in me the seed that, "Truth is a pathless land". Also a seed is planted in my consciousness that says, "There is a way to truth, follow me". One is false, one is true. They are both embedded in my consciousness. So there is a struggle going on. The true and the false, both are operating, which causes more confusion, more misery and a great deal of suffering, if I am sensitive enough. If I don't escape from that suffering what takes place?

Dr B: If you don't escape, then it's clear what will take place. Then you will have the energy to see what is true.

K: That's right.

Dr B: But now let's take the people who do escape, who seem to be a large number.

K : They are out, quite right, millions are out. But still, the struggle is going on.

Dr B: Yes, but it is creating confusion.

K : That is what they are all doing.

Dr B: Yes, but we don't know the outcome of that.

K : Oh yes, we do; dictatorship, deterioration.

Dr B: I know, it gets worse. But now we want to get it clear. In a few people who face the suffering, the energy comes to perceive the truth. And in a large number, who escape from suffering, things get worse.

K : And they rule the world.

Dr B: Now what is the way out of that?

K : They say there is no answer to that, get away from it.

Dr B: That also won't do.

K : They say you can't solve this problem, go away into the mountains or join a monastery, become a monk—but that doesn't solve anything. All one can do is to go on shouting.

Dr B: Yes, then we have to say we don't know the outcome of the shouting.

K : If you shout in order to get an outcome, it is not the right kind of shouting.

Dr B: Yes, that is the situation.

K : You talk, you point out. If nobody wants to pay attention it's their business, you just go on.

45

Now I want to go further. You see, there is a mystery; thought cannot touch it. What is the point of it?

Dr B: Of the mystery? I think you could see it like this: that if you look into the field of thought and reason and so on, you finally see it has no clear foundation. Therefore you see that "what is" must be beyond that. "What is" is the mystery.

K: Yes.

Dr B: I mean, you cannot live in this field of reality and thought, because of all we said.

K: No, of course not. But I don't mind, I have no fears.

Dr B: You don't mind because you have psychological security. Even if something happens to you, it does not deeply affect you.

K: I live in the field of reality, that is my life. There I am consciously aware, and I struggle and keep going in that field. And I can never touch the other. I cannot say, "I can touch it"; there is no "I" to touch it when you really touch it.

You say to me, "There is a mystery which passes all understanding". Because I am caught in *this*, I would like to get *that*. You say there is a mystery, because to you it is an actuality, not an invention, not a superstition, not self-deception. It is truth to you. And what you say makes a tremendous impression on me, because of your integrity. You point it out to me and I would like to get it. Somehow I must get it. What is your responsibility to me?

You understand the position? You say words cannot touch it, thought cannot touch it, no action can touch it, only the action of truth; perhaps it will give you a feeling of that. And I, because I am a miserable human being, would like to get some of that. But you say, "Truth is a pathless land, don't follow anybody"—and I am left.

I realise, I am consciously aware of the limitation of

46

thought, of all the confusion, misery, and all the rest of it. Somehow I can't get out of it. Is your compassion going to help me? You are compassionate, because part of that extraordinary mystery *is* compassion. Will your compassion help me?—obviously not.

So what am I to do? I have a consuming desire for that, and you say, "Don't have any desire, you can't have that, it isn't your personal property". All you say to me is : put order into the field of reality.

Dr B: Yes, and do not escape suffering.

K : If you actually put order into the field of reality then something will take place. And also you say to me, it must be done instantly.

Is that mystery something everybody knows?—knows in the sense that there is something mysterious. Not the desire that creates mysteries, but that there is something mysterious in life apart from my suffering, apart from my death, from my jealousy, my anxiety. Apart from all that, there is a feeling that there is a great mystery in life. Is that it?—that there is a mystery which each one knows?

Dr B: I should think that in some sense everybody knows it. Probably one is born with that sense and it gradually gets dimmed through the conditioning.

K : And has he got the vitality, or the intensity, to put away all that? You see, that means "God is within you"—that is the danger of it.

Dr B: Not exactly, but there is some sort of intimation of this. I think probably children have it more strongly when they are young.

K : Do you think that modern children have that?

Dr B: I don't know about them, probably less. You see, living in a modern city must have a bad effect.

K : Of course.

Dr B: There are many causes. One is lack of contact with nature; I think any contact with nature gives that sense of mystery.

K : Yes.

Dr B: If you look at the sky at night, for example.

K : But you see the scientists are explaining the stars.

Dr B: Yes, I understand that.

K : Cousteau explains the ocean; everything is being explained away.

Dr B: Yes, the feeling has been created that in principle we could know everything.

K : So knowledge is becoming the curse. You see, perception has nothing to do with knowledge. Truth and knowledge don't go together; knowledge cannot contain the immensity of mystery.

Dr B: Yes, I think if we start with a little child, he may place the mystery in some part that he doesn't know. He could put it at the bottom of the ocean, or somewhere else outside, far away from where he is, and then he learns that people have been everywhere. Therefore the whole thing is made to appear non-existent.

K : Yes. Everything becomes so superficial.

Dr B: That's the danger of our modern age, that it gives the appearance that we know more or less everything. At least that we have a general idea of the scheme, if not of the details.

K : The other night I was listening to Bronowski, "The Ascent of Man". He explains everything.

Dr B: The original impulse was to penetrate into this mystery, that was the impulse of science. And somehow it has gone astray. It gives the appearance of explaining it.

K : May I ask, do you as a trained scientist get the feeling of this mystery?

Dr B: I think so, yes. But I've always had some of that, you see.

K : But in talking now, do you get more of the intensity of it? Not because I feel intense, that's a totally different thing, that then becomes influence and all that. But in talking about something we open a door.

Dr B: Yes. I think that my particular conditioning has a great deal in it to resist this notion of mystery, although I think that science is now going in a wrong direction.

K : But even the scientists admit that there is a mystery.

Dr B: Yes, to some extent. The general view is that it could be eventually cleared up.

K : Cleared up in the sense of explained away.

Dr B: My own feeling is that every particular scientific explanation will be a certain part of this field of reality, and therefore will not clear away the mystery.

K : No, but it clears it away because I listen to you explaining everything, and then I say, "There is nothing".

Dr B: That is the main point of distinguishing between truth and reality, because we could say, in the field of reality we may explain more and more broadly without limit.

K : That is what the present day Communists are doing.

Dr B: Not only the Communists.

K : Of course not, I'm taking that as an example.

Dr B: I think you could say, anything in the field of reality can be explained, we can penetrate more deeply and broadly, there is limitless progress possible. But the essence is not explained.

K : No, I am asking a different question, I'm asking you, in talking like this, do you have an intimation of that mystery. Being a scientist, a serious person, perhaps you had an intimation long ago. In talking now, do you feel it's no longer an intimation but a truth?

Dr B: Yes, it is a truth.

K : So it's no longer an intimation?

Dr B: I think it's been a truth for some time now. Because it's implied in what we have been doing here at Brockwood.

K : Yes. You see there is something interesting : the truth of that mystery makes the mind completely empty, doesn't it—? it's completely silent. Or because it is silent, the truth of that mystery *is*.

I don't know if I'm conveying anything. When the mind is completely silent, not in use, not meditated upon, and because it has put order in reality it is free from that confusion, there is a certain silence, the mind is just moving away from confusion. Realising that is not silence, not moving away from that realisation but staying with it, means negating that which order has produced.

Dr B: You say, first you produce order. Why is it necessary to produce the order first and then negate it?

K : To negate is silence.

Dr B: This is why it has to take place in that sequence.

K: Because when I remove disorder there is a certain mathematical order, and as a result of that order my mind is quiet.

Dr B: You say that is not a true silence.

K: No. Realising that is not true silence I negate the false silence, for the moment. So in the negation of that silence I don't want any other silence. There is no movement towards greater silence. Then this total silence opens the door to that. That is, when the mind, with all the confusion, is nothing—not a thing—then perhaps there is the other.

PART II

Talks and Dialogues

Chapter 4

RIGHT ACTION

"You cannot go through reality to come to truth; you must understand the limitation of reality, which is the whole process of thought."

WE MUST ALL be very concerned with what is going on in the world. The disintegration, the violence, the brutality, the wars and the dishonesty in high political places. In the face of this disintegration what is correct action? What is one to do to survive in freedom and be totally religious? We are using the word "religious" not in the orthodox sense, which is not religious. The meaning of that word is: gathering together all energy to find out what is the place of thought and where are its limitations and to go beyond it. That is the true significance and the meaning of that world "religious". So what is one to do in this disintegrating, corrupt, immoral world, as a human being—not an individual, because there is no such thing as the individual—we are human beings, we are collective, not individual, we are the result of various collective influences, forces, conditioning and so on. As human beings, whether we live in this country, or in America or in Russia or in India, which is going through terrible times, what is one to do? What is the correct, right action? To find this out, if one is at all serious—and I hope we are serious here, otherwise you wouldn't have come—what is one to do? Is there an action that is total, whole, not fragmented, that is both correct and accurate, that is compassionate, religious in the sense we are using that word? This has nothing whatsoever to do with

55

belief, dogma, ritual, or the conditioning of a certain type of religious enquiry. What is a human being confronted with this problem to do?

To find an answer, not imaginary, fictitious or pretended, to find the true, the right answer one must enquire into the whole movement of thought. Because all our conditioning, all our activity, all our political, economic, social, moral and religious life is based on thought. Thought has been our chief instrument in all the fields of life, in all the areas, religious, moral, political, economic, social, and in personal relationships: I think that is fairly obvious. Please, if I may point out, we are talking this over together. We are enquiring into this together, sharing it, your responsibility is to share it, not just merely listen to a few ideas, agree or disagree, but to share it; which means you must give attention to it, you must care for it, this problem must be serious, this problem must be something that touches your mind, your heart, everything in life—otherwise there is no sharing, there is no communion, there is no communication except verbally or intellectually and that has very little value. So we are together enquiring into this question.

What is the responsibility of thought?—knowing its limitation, knowing that whatever it does is within a limited area; and in that limited area is it possible to have correct, accurate response and action? At what level does one find for oneself, as a human being, the right action? If it is imaginary, personal, according to an idea, a concept, or an ideal, it ceases to be correct action. I hope we are understanding each other. The ideal, the conclusion is still the movement of thought as time, as measure. And thought has created all our problems; in our personal relationships, economically, socially, morally, religiously, thought has not found an answer. And we are trying to find out if we can, this morning—and in the next two or three talks—what is the action which is whole, non-traditional, non-mechanistic, which is not a conclusion, a prejudice, a belief. That is, I want to find out, if I am at all

serious, how am I to act? An action in which there is no pretension, an action that has no regrets, an action that does not
breed further problems, an action that will be whole, complete
and answer every issue, whether at the personal level, or at the
most complex social level. I hope this is your problem. Unless
we solve this problem very deeply, talking about meditation,
about what is God, what is truth and all the rest of it, has
very little meaning. One must lay the foundation, otherwise
one cannot go very far. One must begin as close as possible to
go very far, and the nearness is you, as a human being living
in this monstrous, corrupt society. And one must find for oneself an action that is whole, non-fragmented, because the world
is becoming more and more dangerous to live in, it is becoming a desert and each one of us has to be an oasis. To bring
about that—not an isolated existence—but a total human
existence, our enquiry is into the problem of action.

Can thought solve our problems, thought being the response
of memory, experience and knowledge? Memory is a material
process; thought is material and chemical—the scientists agree
about this. And the things that thought has created in the world
and in ourselves is the world of reality, the world of things.
Reality means the thing that exists. And to find out what
truth is one must be very clear where the limitations of reality
are, and not let it flow into the world that is not real.

One observes in the world and in oneself, thought has created
an extraordinary complex problem of existence. Thought has
created the centre as the "me" and the "you". And from that
centre we act. Please look at it, observe it, you will see it for
yourself; you are not accepting something the speaker is talking
about, don't accept anything. You know, when one begins to
doubt everything, then from that doubt, from that uncertainty
grows certainty, clarity; but if you start with imagination,
belief, and live within that area you will end up always doubt-
ing. Here we are trying to investigate, enquire, look into things
that are very close to us: which is our daily life, with all its

misery, conflict, pain, suffering, love and anxiety, greed, envy, all that.

As we said, thought has created the "me", and so thought in itself being fragmentary makes the me into a fragment. When you say "I", "me", "I want, I don't want, I am this, I am not that", it is the result of thought. And thought itself being fragmentary, thought is never the whole, so what it has created becomes fragmentary. "My world", "my religion", "my belief", "my country", "my god" and yours, so it becomes fragmentary. Thought intrinsically is a process of time, measure, and therefore fragmentary. I wonder if you see this? If you see this once very clearly, then we will be able to find out what is action, a correct, accurate action in which there is no imagination, no pretension, nothing but the actual.

We are trying to find out what is action that is whole, that is not fragmentary, that is not caught in the movement of time, not traditional and therefore mechanical. One wants to live a life without conflict and live in a society that doesn't destroy freedom, and yet survive. As the societies and governments throughout the world are becoming more and more centralised, more and more bureaucratic, our freedom is getting less and less. Freedom is not what one likes to do, what one wants to do, that is not freedom. Freedom means something entirely different. It means freedom from this constant battle, constant anxiety, uncertainty, suffering, pain, all the things that thought has created in us.

Now is there an action which is not based on the mechanical process of memory, on a repetition of an experience and therefore a continuing in the movement of time as past, present and future? Is there an action that is not conditioned by environment? You know the Marxists say that if you control the environment then you will change man, and that has been tried and man has not changed. Man remains primitive, vulgar, cruel, brutal, violent and all the rest of it, though they are controlling the environment. And there are those who say don't bother about the environment, but believe in some divinity and that will guide you; and that divinity is the projection of thought. So we are back again in the same field. Realising all this what is a human being to do?

Can thought, which is a material, a chemical process, a thing, which has created all this structure, can that very thought solve our problems? One must very carefully, diligently, find out what are the limitations of thought. And can thought itself realise its limitation and therefore not spill over into the realm which thought can never touch? Thought has created the technological world, and thought has also created the division between "you" and "me". Thought has created the image of you and the "me" and these images separate each one of us. Thought can only function in duality, in opposites, and therefore all reaction is a divisive process, a separative process. And thought has created division between human beings, nationalities, religious beliefs, dogmas, political differences, opinions, conclusions, all that is the result of thought. Thought has also created the division between you and me as form and name; and thought has created the centre which is the "me" as opposed to you, therefore there is a division between you and me. Thought has created this whole structure of social behaviour, which is essentially based on tradition, which is mechanical. Thought has also created the religious world, the Christian, the Buddhist, the Hindu, the Muslim, with all the divisions, all the practices, all the innumerable gurus that are springing up like mushrooms. And thought has created what it considers is love. Is compassion the result of "love", the result of thought? That is our problem, those are all our problems.

Yet we are trying to solve all these problems through thought. Can thought see itself as the mischief-maker, see itself as a necessary instrument in the creation of a society which is not immoral? Can thought be aware of itself? Please do follow this. Can your thought become conscious of itself?

And if it does, is that consciousness part of thought? One can be aware of the activities of thought, and one can choose between those activities as good and bad, worthwhile and not worthwhile, but the choice is still the result of thought. And therefore it is perpetuating conflict and duality. Can thought be attentive to its own movements? Or is there an entity outside the field of thought which directs thought? I can say I am aware of my thoughts, I know what I am thinking, but that entity which says, "I know what I am thinking", that "I" is the product of thought. And that entity then begins to control, subjugate, or rationalise thinking. So there is an entity, we say, which is different from thought : but it is essentially thought. What we are trying to explain is : thought is tremendously limited, it plays all kinds of tricks, it imagines, it creates a super-consciousness—but it is still thought.

So our problem then is : can thought realise for itself where it is essential to operate, where it is accurate in its operation, and yet totally limited in every other direction? That means, one has to go into this question of human consciousness. This sounds very philosophical, very complicated, but it isn't. Philosophy means the love of truth, not love of words, not love of ideas, not love of speculations, but the love of truth. And that means you have to find out for yourself where reality is and that reality cannot become truth. You cannot go through reality to come to truth. You must understand the limitations of reality, which is the whole process of thought. You know, when you look into yourself, knowing your consciousness, why you think, what your motives are, what your purposes are, your beliefs, your intentions, your pretentions, what your imaginations are, all that is your consciousness; and that consciousness essentially is the consciousness of the world. Please do see this. Your consciousness is not radically different from the consciousness of a Muslim, a Hindu, or anybody else, because your consciousness is filled with anxiety, hope, fear, pleasure, suffering, greed, envy, competition; that is consciousness. Your beliefs and your gods, everything is in that consciousness. The content of that makes up your consciousness, and the content of that is thought—thought that has filled consciousness with the things it has created. Look into yourself and you will see how extraordinary obvious it is.

And from this content, which is conditioned, which is the tradition, which is the result of thought, we are trying to find a way to act within that area—within that area of consciousness which thought has filled with the things of thought. And one asks : if thought cannot solve all our human problems—other than technological or mathematical problems—then how can it limit itself and not enter into the field of the psyche, into the field of the spirit?—we can use that word for the moment. As long as we function within that area we must always suffer, there must always be disorder, there must always be fear and anxiety. So my question is : can I, can a human being bring about order in the world of reality? And when thought has established order in the world of reality, then it will realise its own tremendous limitations. I wonder if you see this? We live in a world of disorder, not only outwardly but inwardly. And we have not been able to solve this disorder. We try everything—meditation, drugs, accepting authority, denying authority, pursuing freedom and denying freedom—we have done everything possible to bring about order—through compulsion, through fear—but we still live in disorder. And a disordered mind is now trying to find out if there is a correct action—you follow? A disordered mind is trying to find out if there is a right, accurate, correct action. And it will find an action which is incorrect, disorderly, not whole. Therefore in the world of reality in which we live we must bring about order. I wonder if you see this?

Order is not the acceptance of authority. Order is not what one wants to do. Order is not something according to a blueprint. Order must be something highly mathematical, the greatest mathematical order is the total denial of disorder, and so within oneself, within the human being. Can you look at your disorder, be aware of it, not choosing particular forms of disorder, accepting some and denying others, but see the whole disorder? Disorder implies conflict, self-centred activity, the acceptance of a conclusion and living according to that conclusion, the ideal and the pursuit of the ideal which denies the actual; can you totally deny all that? It is only when you deny totally all that, that there is order, the order that is not created by thought in the world of reality. You understand? We are separating reality and truth. We say reality is everything that thought has created; and in that area, in that field, there is total disorder, except in the world of technology. In that field human beings live in complete disorder and this disorder is brought about, as we have explained, by conflict, by the pursuit of pleasure, fear, suffering, all that. Can you become aware of all that and totally deny it—walk away from it? Out of that comes order in the world of reality.

In that world of reality behaviour is something entirely different. When you have denied all that, denied the "me", which is the product of thought, which creates the division, the thought that has created the "me" and the super-conscious, all the imaginations, the pretentions, the anxieties, the acceptance and the denial. That is the content which is so traditional; to deny that tradition is to have order. Then we can go into the question of what truth is, not before; otherwise it becomes pretentious, hypocritical, nonsensical. In that one has to understand the whole question of fear, how human beings live in fear, and that fear is now becoming more and more acute, because the world is becoming so dangerous a place, where tyrannies are increasing, political tyrannies, bureaucratic tyrannies, denying freedom for the mind to understand, to enquire.

So can we as human beings, living in this disorderly, disintegrating world, become actually, not in theory or imagination, an oasis in a world that is becoming a desert? This is really a very serious question. And can we human beings educate ourselves totally differently? We can do that only if we understand the nature and the movement of thought as time, which means really understanding oneself as a human being. To look at ourselves not according to some psychologist, but to look at ourselves actually as we are and discover how disorderly a life we lead—a life of uncertainty, a life of pain, living on conclusions, beliefs, memories. And becoming aware of it, that very awareness washes away all this.

For the rest of this morning can we talk over together, by question and enquiry, what we have talked about? Please, you are asking questions not of me, not of the speaker. We are asking questions of ourselves, saying it aloud so that we can all share it because your problem is the problem of everybody else. Your problem is the problem of the world, you are the world. I don't think we realise that. You are actually the world, in the very deepest essence—your manners, your dress, your name and your form may be different—but essentially, deep down, you are the world, you have created the world and the world is you. So if you ask a question you are asking it for the whole of mankind. I don't know if you see that?— which doesn't mean that you mustn't ask questions, on the contrary. Questioning then becomes a very serious matter, not a glib question and a glib answer, some momentary question and forget it till another day. If you ask, ask about a really human problem.

Questioner: Did you say that by walking away from the disorder of traditions we create order? Is that what you meant?

KRISHNAMURTI: Yes, that is what I meant. Now just a minute, that needs a great deal of explanation of what you mean by tradition, what you mean by walking away, what you mean by order.

Q: In addition to that question, the seeing of this disorder already implies that the 'see-er' has gone, that you have walked away.

K : There are three things involved in this : order, walking away, and the observation of disorder. Walking away from disorder, the very act of moving away from it, is order. Now first, how do you observe disorder? How do you observe disorder in yourself? Are you looking at it as an outsider looking in, as something separate and there is therefore a division, you and the thing which you are observing? Or are you looking at it, if I may ask, not as an outsider, without the outsider, without the observer who says, "I am disorderly"? Let us put it round the other way. When you look at something, those trees and that house, there is a space between you and that tree and that house. The space is the distance and you must have a certain distance to look, to observe. If you are too close you don't see the whole thing. So if you are an observer looking at disorder, there is a space between you and that disorder. Then the problem arises, how to cover that space, how to control that disorder, how to rationalise the disorder, how to suppress it, or whatever you do. But if there is no space you *are* that disorder. I wonder if you see that?

Q: How can I walk away from it?

K : I am going to show it to you; I am going to go into that. You understand my question?

When you observe your wife, your husband, a boy or a girl—nowadays they don't marry—or your friend, how do you observe him or her? Watch it please. Go into it, it is very simple. Do you observe directly, or do you observe that person through an image, through a screen, from a distance? Obviously, if you have lived with a person—it doesn't matter if it's for a day or ten years—there is an image, a distance. You are separate from her or him. And when you observe disorder you have an image of what order is; or an image which says, "this disorder is ugly". So you are looking at that disorder from a distance, which is time, which is tradition, which is the past. And is that distance created by thought? Or does this distance actually exist? When you say, "I am angry", is anger different from you? No, so you *are* anger. You are disorderly : not you separate from disorder. I think that is clear.

So you are that disorder. Any movement—please follow this—any movement of thought away from that disorder is still disorder. Because that disorder is created by thought. That disorder is the result of your self-centred activity, the centre that says, "I am different from somebody else" and so on. All that produces disorder. Now can you observe that disorder without the observer?

Q: Then you will find in yourself what you are criticising in the other?

K : No, no. I am not talking about criticising the others. That has very little meaning, criticising others.

Q: No, what you found in the other, you will find it in yourself.

K : No, madam. The other is me; essentially the other is me. He has his anxieties, his fears, his hopes, his despairs, his suffering, his pain, his loneliness, his misery, his lack of love and all the rest of it; that man or women is me. If that is clear, then I am not criticising another, I am aware of myself in the other.

Q: That is what I meant.

K : Good. So is there an observation without the past, the past being the observer? Can you look at me, or look at another, without all the memories, all the chicanery, all the things that go on—just look? Can you look at your husband, wife and so on, without a single image? Can you look at another without the whole past springing up? You do, when there is an absolute crisis. When there is a tremendous challenge you do look that way. But we live such sloppy lives, we are not serious, we don't work.

Q: How can you live permanently at crisis pitch?

K : I'll answer that question, sir, after we have finished this.

So the walking away from it is to be totally involved in that which you observe. And when I observe this disorder without all the reactions, the memories, the things that crop up in one's mind, then in that total observation, that very total observation is order. I wonder if you see this? Which raises the question, have you ever looked at anything totally? Have you looked at your political leaders, your religious beliefs, your conclusions, the whole thing on which we live, which is thought, have you looked at it completely? And to look at it completely means no division between you and that which looks. I can look at a mountain and the beauty of it, the line of it, the shadows, the depth, the dignity, the marvellous isolation and beauty of it, and it is not a process of identification. I cannot become the mountain, thank God! That is a trick of the imagination. But when I observe without the word "mountain", I see there is a perception of that beauty entirely. A passion comes out of that. And can I observe another, my wife, friend, child, whoever it is, can I observe totally? That means can I observe without the observer who is the past? Which means observation implies total perception. There is only perception, not the perceiver. Then there is order.

Q: If there is only perception and no perceiver, what is it that looks? If I see that I am disorder, what is it that sees it?

K : Now go into it, sir. Disorder is a large word, let us look at it. When you see that you are violent and that violence is not different from you, that you are that violence—what takes place? Let us look at it round the other way.

What takes place when you are not the violence? You say

66

violence is different from "me", what happens then? In that there is division, in that there is trying to control violence, in that there is a projection of a state of non-violence, the ideal, and conformity to that ideal; therefore further conflict, and so on. So when there is a division between the observer and the observed, the sequence is a continuous conflict in different varieties and shapes; but when the observer *is* the observed, that is when the observer says, "I am violent, the violence is not separate from 'me' ", then a totally different kind of activity takes place. There is no conflict, there is no rationalisation, there is no suppression, control, there is no non-violence as an ideal: you are that. Then what takes place? I don't know if you have ever gone into this question.

Q: Then what is "you"? One cannot speak without "you".

K: No, madam, that is a way of speaking. Look, please. You see the difference between the observer and the observed. When there is a difference between the observer and the observed there must be conflict in various forms because there is division. When there is a political division, when there is a national division there must be conflict; as is going on in the world. Where there is division there must be conflict; that is law. And when the observer is the observed, when violence is not separate from the observer, then a totally different action takes place. The word "violence" is already condemnatory; it is a word we use in order to strengthen violence, though we may not want to, we strengthen it by using that word, don't we? So the naming of that feeling is part of our tradition. If you don't name it then there is a totally different response. And because you don't name it, because there is no observer different from the observed, then the feeling that arises, which you call violence, is non-existent. You try it and you will see it. You can only act when you test it. But mere agreement is not testing it. You have to act and find out.

The next question was about challenge. Must we always live with challenge?

Q: I said crisis.

K : Crisis, it is the same thing. Aren't you living in crisis? There is a political crisis in this country, an economic crisis, crisis with your wife or your husband; crisis means division, doesn't it? Which means crisis apparently becomes necessary for those people who live in darkness, who are asleep. If you had no crisis you would all go to sleep. And that is what we want—"For God's sake leave me alone!"—to wallow in my own little pond, or whatever it is. But crisis comes all the time.

Now a much deeper question is : is it possible to live without a single crisis and keep totally awake? You understand? Crisis, challenge, shock, disturbance exist when the mind is sluggish, traditional, repetitive, unclear. Can the mind become completely clear, and therefore to such a mind there is no challenge? Is that possible?

That means, we have to go deeper still. We live on experiences to change our minds, to further our minds, to enlarge our minds; experiences, we think will create, will open the door to clarity. And we think a man who has no experience is asleep, or dull or stupid. A man who has no experience, but is fully awake, has an innocent mind, therefore he sees clearly. Now is that possible? Don't say yes or no.

Q: When you say he has no experience, do you mean in the sense that he is ignorant of basic life?

K : No, no. Sir, look. We are conditioned by the society in which we live, by the food we eat, clothes, climate. We are conditioned by the culture, by the literature, by the newspapers, our mind is shaped by everything, consciously, or unconsciously. When you call yourself a Christian, a Buddhist, or whatever it is, that is your conditioning. And we move from one conditioning to another. I don't like Hinduism so I jump into Christianity, or into something else. If I don't like one guru I just follow another guru. So we are conditioned. Is it possible to uncondition the mind so that it is totally free? That means is it possible to be aware of your total conditioning—not choose which conditionings you like, but total conditioning, which is only possible when there is no choice and when there is no observer. To see the whole of that conditioning, which is at both the conscious level as well as at the unconscious level, the totality of it! And you can see the totality of something only when there is no distance between you and that—the distance created as movement of thought, time. Then you see the whole of it. And when there is a perception of the whole, then the unconditioning comes into being. But we don't want to work at that kind of thing. We want the easiest way with everything. That is why we like gurus. The priest, the politician, the authority, the specialist, they know, but we don't know; they will tell us what to do, which is our traditional acceptance of authority.

Q: A question about true action. Actually, as we are, every action is a self-centred activity. So when you see that, you are afraid to act because everything has no significance. That is a reality, there is no choice or imagination. You are facing a terrible void and you . . .

K : I understand the question . . .

Q: Even material activity.

K : When there is an observation and you see you can't do anything, then you say there is a void. Just hold on to that sentence, to that phrase. There is an observation, you realise you can't do anything and therefore there is a void. Is that so? When I see that I have been able to do something before, there was no void. You understand? I could do something about it, join the Liberal Party, become a neurotic or whatever it is—sorry! (*Laughter*). Before I could do something and I thought by doing something there was no void. Because I had filled the void by doing something, which is running away from that void, that loneliness, that extraordinary sense of isolation. And now when I see the falseness of this doing, a doing about something—which doesn't give a significance or an answer—then I say to myself, "I observe that I am the observer, and I am left naked, stark naked, void. I can't do anything. There is no significance to existence." Before, you gave significance to existence, which is the significance created by thought, by all kinds of imaginings, hope and all the rest of it, and suddenly you realise that thought doesn't solve the problems and you see no meaning in life, no significance. So you want to give significance to life—you understand? You want to *give* it. (*Laughter*). No, don't laugh, this is what we are doing. Living itself has no meaning for most of us now. When we are young we say, "Well at least I'll be happy"—sex and all the rest of it. As we grow older we say, "My God, it is such an empty life", and you fill that emptiness with literature, with knowledge, with beliefs, dogmas, rituals, opinions, judgements, and you think that has tremendous significance. You have filled it with words, nothing else but words. Now when you strip yourself of words you say, "I am empty, void".

Q: These are still words.

K : Still words, that is what I am saying. Still words. So when you see that thought has created what you considered to be significance, now when you see the limitation of thought, and that what it has created has no significance, you are left empty, void, naked. Why? Aren't you still seeking something? Isn't thought still in operation? When you say, "I have no significance, there is no significance to life", it is thought that has made you say there is no significance, because you want significance. But when there is no movement of thought, life is full of significance. It has tremendous beauty. You don't know of this.

Q: Thought is afraid not to think.

K : So thought is afraid not to think. We will go into that tomorrow : the whole problem of thought creating fear and trying to give significance to life. If one actually examines one's life, there is very little meaning, is there? You have pleasant memories or unpleasant memories, which is in the past, dead, gone, but you hold on to them. There is all this fear of death. You have worked and worked and worked—God knows why—and there is that thing waiting for you. And you say, "Is that all?" So we have to go into this question of the movement of thought as time and measure.

Chapter 5

THE PROBLEM OF FEAR

"If you can be totally free of fear, then heaven is with you."

W E M U S T B E serious in facing what we have to do in life, with all the problems, miseries, confusion, violence and suffering. Only those live who are really earnest, but the others fritter their life away and waste their existence. We were going to consider this morning the whole complex problem of fear. The human mind has lived so long, so many centuries upon centuries, putting up with fear, escaping from it, trying to rationalise it, trying to forget it, or completely identifying with something that is not fear—we have tried all these methods. And one asks if it is at all possible to be free totally, completely of fear, psychologically and from that physiologically. We are going to discuss this, talk it over together, and find out for ourselves if it is at all possible.

First, we must consider energy, the quality of energy, the types of energy, and the question of desire; and whether we have sufficient energy to delve deeply into this question. We know the energy and friction of thought; it has created most extraordinary things in the world technologically. But psychologically we don't seem to have that deep energy, drive, interest to penetrate profoundly into this question of fear.

We have to understand this question of thought bringing about its own energy and therefore a fragmentary energy, an energy through friction, through conflict. That is all we know: the energy of thought, the energy that comes through contradiction, through opposition in duality, the energy of friction.

72

All that is in the world of reality, reality being the things with which we live daily, both psychologically and intellectually and so on.

I hope we can communicate with each other. Communication implies not only verbal understanding, but actually sharing what is being said, otherwise there is no communion. There is not only a verbal communication but a communion which is non-verbal. But to come to that non-verbal communion, one must understand very deeply whether it is possible to communicate with each other at a verbal level, which means that both of us share the meaning of the words, have the same interest, the same intensity, at the same level, so that we can proceed step by step. That requires energy. And that energy can come into being only when we understand the energy of thought and its friction, in which we are caught. If you investigate into yourself you will see that what we know, or experience, is the friction of thought in its achievement, in its desires, in its purposes—the striving, the struggle, the competition. All that is involved in the energy of thought.

Now we are asking if there is any other kind of energy, which is not mechanistic, not traditional, non-contradictory, and therefore without the tension that creates energy. To find that out, whether there is another kind of energy, not imagined, not fantastic, not superstitious, we have to go into the question of desire.

Desire is the want of something, isn't it? That is one fragment of desire. Then there is the longing for something, whether it be sexual longing or psychological longing, or so-called spiritual longing. And how does this desire arise? Desire is the want of something, the lack of something, missing something; then the longing for it, either imaginatively, or actual want, like hunger; and there is the problem of how desire arises in one. Because, in coming face to face with fear, we have to understand desire—not the denial of desire, but insight into desire. Desire may be the root of fear. The religious

73

monks throughout the world have denied desire, they have resisted desire, they have identified that desire with their gods, with their saviours, with their Jesus, and so on. But it is still desire. And without the full penetration into that desire, without having an insight into it, one's mind cannot possibly be free from fear.

We need a different kind of energy, not the mechanistic energy of thought, because that has not solved any of our problems; on the contrary, it has made them much more complex, more vast, impossible to solve. So we must find a different kind of energy, whether that energy is related to thought or is independent of thought, and in enquiring into that one must go into the question of desire. You are following this?—not somebody else's desire, but your own desire. Now how does desire arise? One can see that this movement of desire takes place through perception, then sensation, contact and so desire. One sees something beautiful, the contact of it, visual and physical, sensory, then sensation, then from that the feeling of the lack of it. And from that desire. That is fairly clear.

Why does the mind, the whole sensory organism, lack? Why is there this feeling of lacking something, of wanting something? I hope you are giving sufficient attention to what is being said, because it is your life. You are not merely listening to words, or ideas, or formulas, but actually sharing in the investigating process so that we are together walking in the same direction, at the same speed, with the same intensity, at the same level. Otherwise we shan't meet each other. That is part of love also. Love is that communication with each other, at the same level, at the same time, with the same intensity.

So why is there the sense of lacking or wanting in oneself? I do not know if you have ever gone into this question at all? Why the human mind, or human beings, are always after something—apart from technological knowledge, apart from

learning languages and so on and so on, why is there this
sense of wanting, lacking, pursuing something all the time?—
which is the movement of desire, which is also the movement
of thought in time, as time and measure. All that is involved.

We are asking, why there is this sense of want. Why there is
not a sense of complete self-sufficiency? Why is there this longing for something in order to fulfil or to cover up something?
Is it because for most of us there is a sense of emptiness, loneliness, a sense of void? Physiologically we need food, clothes
and shelter, that one must have. But that is denied when there
is political, religious, economic division, nationalistic division,
which is the curse of this world, which has been invented by
the Western world, it did not exist in the Eastern world, this
spirit of nationality; it has come recently into being there too,
this poison. And when there is division between peoples,
between nationalities and between beliefs, dogmas, security
for everybody becomes almost impossible. The tyrannical
world of dictatorship is trying to provide that, food for everybody, but it cannot achieve it. We know all that, we can move
from that. So what is it that we lack? Knowledge?—knowledge being the accumulation of experience, psychological,
scientific and in other directions, which is knowledge in the
past. Knowledge is the past. Is this what we want? Is this
what we miss? Is this what we are educated for, to gather all
the knowledge we can possibly have, to act skilfully in the
technological world? Or is there a sense of lack, want, psychologically, inwardly? Which means you will try to fill that
inward emptiness, that lack, through or with experience, which
is the accumulated knowledge. So you are trying to fill that
emptiness, that void, that sense of immense loneliness, with
something which thought has created. Therefore desire arises
from this urge to fill that emptiness. After all, when you are
seeking enlightenment, or self-realisation as the Hindus call it,
it is a form of desire. This sense of ignorance will be wiped
away, or put aside, or dissipated by acquiring tremendous

knowledge, enlightenment. It is never the process of investigating "what is", but rather of acquiring; not actually looking at "what is", but inviting something which might be, or hopeful of a greater experience, greater knowledge. So we are always avoiding "what is". And the "what is" is created by thought. My loneliness, emptiness, sorrow, pain, suffering, anxiety, fear, that is actually "what is". And thought is incapable of facing it and tries to move away from it.

So in the understanding of desire—that is perception, seeing, contact, sensation, and the want of that which you have not, and so desire, the longing for it—that involves the whole process of time. I have not, but I will have. And when I do have it is measured by what you have. So desire is the movement of thought in time as measure. Please don't just agree with me. I am not interested in doing propaganda. I don't care if you are here or not here, if you listen or don't listen. But as it is your life, as it is so urgently important that we be deadly serious—the world is disintegrating—you have to understand this question of desire, energy, and the enquiry into a different kind of non-mechanical energy. And to come to that you must understand fear. That is, does desire create fear? We are going to enquire together into this question of fear, what is fear? You may say, "Well let's forget about energy and desire and please help me to get rid of my fear"— that is too silly, they are all related. You can't take one thing and approach it that way. You must take the whole packet.

So what is fear, how does it arise? Is there a fear at one level and not at another level? Is there fear at the conscious level or at the unconscious level? Or is there a fear totally? Now how does fear arise? Why does it exist in human beings? And human beings have put up with it for generations upon generations, they live with it. Fear distorts action, distorts clear perceptive thinking, objective efficient thinking, which is necessary, logical sane healthy thinking. Fear darkens our lives. I do not know if you have noticed it? If there is the slightest fear there is a contraction of all our senses. And most of us live, in whatever relationship we have, in that peculiar form of fear.

Our question is, whether the mind and our whole being can ever be free completely of fear. Education, society, governments, religions have encouraged this fear; religions are based on fear. And fear also is cultivated through the worship of authority—the authority of a book, the authority of the priest, the authority of those who know and so on. We are carefully nurtured in fear. And we are asking whether it is at all possible to be totally free of it. So we have to find out what is fear. Is it the want of something?—which is desire, longing. Is it the uncertainty of tomorrow? Or the pain and the suffering of yesterday? Is it this division between you and me, in which there is no relationship at all? Is it that centre which thought has created as the "me"—the me being the form, the name, the attributes—fear of loosing that "me"? Is that one of the causes of fear? Or is it the remembrance of something past, pleasant, happy, and the fear of losing it? Or the fear of suffering, physiologically and psychologically? Is there a centre from which all fear springs?—like a tree, though it has got a hundred branches it has a solid trunk and roots, and it is no good merely pruning the branches. So we have to go to the very root of fear. Because if you can be totally free of fear, then heaven is with you.

What is the root of it? Is it time? Please we are investigating, questioning, we are not theorising, we are not coming to any conclusion, because there is nothing to conclude. The moment you see the root of it, actually, with your eyes, with your feeling, with your heart, with your mind—actually see it—then you can deal with it; that is if you are serious. We are asking : is it time?—time being not only chronological time by the watch, as yesterday, today and tomorrow, but also psychological time, the remembrance of yesterday, the pleasures of yesterday, and the pains, the grief, the anxieties of yesterday.

We are asking whether the root of fear is time. Time to fulfil, time to become, time to achieve, time to realise God, or whatever you like to call it. Psychologically, what is time? Is there such a thing—please listen—as psychological time at all? Or have we invented psychological time? Psychologically is there tomorrow? If one says there is no time psychologically as tomorrow, it will be a great shock to you, won't it? Because you say, "Tomorrow I shall be happy; tomorrow I will achieve something; tomorrow I will become the executive of some business; tomorrow I will become the enlightened one; tomorrow the guru promises something and I'll achieve it". To us tomorrow is tremendously important. And is there a tomorrow psychologically? We have accepted it: that is our whole traditional education, that there is a tomorrow. And when you look psychologicaly, investigate into yourself, is there a tomorrow? Or has thought, being fragmentary in itself, projected the tomorrow? Please, we will go into this, it is very important to understand.

One suffers physically, there is a great deal of pain. And the remembrance of that pain is marked, is an experience which the brain contains and therefore there is the remembrance of that pain. And thought says, "I hope I never have that pain again" : that is tomorrow. There has been great pleasure yesterday, sexual or whatever kind of pleasure one has, and thought says, "Tomorrow I must have that pleasure again". You have a great experience—at least you think it is a great experience—and it has become a memory; and you realise it is a memory yet you pursue it tomorrow. So thought is movement in time. Is the root of fear time?—time as comparison with you, "me" more important than you, "me" that is going to achieve something, become something, get rid of something.

So thought as time, thought as becoming, is the root of fear. We have said that time is necessary to learn a language, time is necessary to learn any technique. And we think we can apply the same process to psychological existence. I need several weeks to learn a language, and I say in order to learn about myself, what I am, what I have to achieve, I need time. We are questioning the whole of that. Whether there is time at all psychologically, actually; or is it an invention of thought and therefore fear arises? That is our problem; and consciously we have divided consciousness into the conscious and the hidden. Again division by thought. And we say, "I may be able to get rid of conscious fears, but it is almost impossible to be free of the unconscious fears with their deep roots in the unconscious". We say that it is much more difficult to be free of unconscious fears, that is the racial fears, the family fears, the tribal fears, the fears that are deeply rooted, instinctive. We have divided consciousness into two levels and then we ask : how can a human being delve into the unconscious? Having divided it then we ask this question.

It is said it can be done through careful analysis of the various hidden fears, through dreams. That is the fashion. We never look into the whole process of analysis, whether it be self-introspective, or professional. In analysis is implied the analyser and the analysed. Who is the analyser? Is he different from the analysed, or is the analyser the analysed? And therefore it is utterly futile to analyse. I wonder if you see that? If the analyser is the analysed, then there is only observation, not analysis. But the analyser as different from the analysed— that is what you all accept, all the professionals, all the people who are trying to improve themselves—God forbid!—they all accept that there is a division between the analysed and the analyser. But the analyser is a fragment of thought which has created that thing to be analysed. I wonder if you follow this? So in analysis is implied a division and that division implies time. And you have to keep on analysing until you die.

So where analysis is totally false—I am using the word "false" in the sense of incorrect, having no value—then you are only concerned with observation. To observe!—we have

to understand what is observation. You are following all this?
We started out by enquiring if there is a different kind of
energy. I am sorry we must go back so that it is in your mind
—not in your memory, then you could read a book and repeat
it to yourself, which is nothing. So we are concerned with, or
enquiring into energy. We know the energy of thought which
is mechanical, a process of friction, because thought in its very
nature is fragmentary, thought is never the whole. And we
have asked if there is a different kind of energy altogether and
we are investigating that. And in enquiring into that we see
the whole movement of desire. Desire is the state of wanting
something, longing for something. And that desire is a movement of thought as time and measure: "I have had this, and
I must have more". And we said in the understanding of fear,
the root of fear may be time as movement. If you go into it
you will see that it is the root of it: that is the actual fact.
Then, is it possible for the mind to be totally free of fear?
For the brain, which has accumulated knowledge, can only
function effectively when there is complete security—but that
security may be in some neurotic activity, in some belief, in
the belief that you are the great nation; and all belief is
neurotic, obviously, because it is not actual. So the brain can
only function effectively, sanely, rationally, when it feels completely secure, and fear does not give it security. To be free of
that fear, we asked whether analysis is necessary. And we see
that analysis does not solve fear. So when you have an insight
into the process of analysis, you stop analysing. And then there
is only the question of observation, seeing. If you don't analyse,
what are you to do? You can only look. And it is very important to find out how to look.

What does it mean to look? What does it mean to look at
this question of desire as movement in time and measure?
How do you see it? Do you see it as an idea, as a formula,
because you have heard the speaker talking about it? Therefore you abstract what you hear into an idea and pursue that

80

idea—which is still looking away from fear. So when you observe, it is very important to find out how you observe.

Can you observe your fear without the movement of escaping, suppressing, rationalising, or giving it a name? That is, can you look at fear, your fear of not having a job tomorrow, of not being loved, a dozen forms of fear, can you look at it without naming, without the observer?—because the observer is the observed. I don't know if you follow this? So the observer *is* fear, not "he" is observing "fear".

Can you observe without the observer?—the observer being the past. Then is there fear? You follow? We have the energy to look at something as an observer. I look at you and say, "You are a Christian, a Hindu, Buddhist", whatever you are, or I look at you saying, "I don't like you", or "I like you". If you believe in the same thing as I believe in you are my friend; if I don't believe the same thing as you do, you are my enemy. So can you look at another without all those movements of thought, of remembrance, of hope, all that, just look? Look at that fear which is the root of time. Then is there fear at all? You understand? You will find this out only if you test it, if you work at it, not just play with it.

Then there is the other form of desire, which not only creates fear but also pleasure. Desire is a form of pleasure. Pleasure is different from joy. Pleasure you can cultivate, which the modern world is doing, sexually and in every form of cultural encouragement—pleasure, tremendous pleasure and the pursuit of pleasure. And in the very pursuit of pleasure there must be fear also, because they are the two sides of the same coin. Joy you cannot invite; if it happens then thought takes charge of it and remembers it and pursues that joy which you had a year ago, or yesterday, and which becomes pleasure. And when there is enjoyment—seeing a beautiful sunset, a lovely tree, or the deep shadow of a lake—then that enjoyment is registered in the brain as memory and the pursuit of that memory is pleasure.

There is fear, pleasure, joy. Is it possible—this is a much more complex problem—is it possible to observe a sunset, the beauty of a person, the lovely shape of an ancient tree in a solitary field, the enjoyment of it, the beauty of it—observe it without registering it in the brain, which then becomes memory, and the pursuit of that tomorrow? That is, to see something beautiful and end it, not carry it on.

There is another principle in man. Besides fear and pleasure, there is the principle of suffering. Is there an end to suffering? We want suffering to end physically, therefore we take drugs and do all kinds of yoga tricks and all that. But we have never been able to solve this question of suffering, human suffering, not only of a particular human being but the suffering of the whole of humanity. There is your suffering, and millions and millions of people in the world are suffering, through war, through starvation, through brutality, through violence, through bombs. And can that suffering in you as a human being end? Can it come to an end in you, because your consciousness is the consciousness of the world, is the consciousness of every other human being? You may have a different peripheral behaviour but basically, deeply, your consciousness is the consciousness of every other human being in the world. Suffering, pleasure, fear, ambition, all that is your consciousness. So you are the world. And if you are completely free of fear you affect the consciousness of the world. Do you understand how extraordinarily important it is that we human beings change, fundamentally, because that will affect the consciousness of every other human being? Hitler, Stalin affected all the consciousness of the world, what the priests have achieved in the name of somebody has affected the world. So if you as human beings radically transform, are free of fear, you will naturally affect the consciousness of the world.

Similarly, when there is freedom from suffering there is compassion, not before. You can talk about it, write books about it, discuss what compassion is, but the ending of sorrow is the beginning of compassion. The human mind has put up with suffering, endless suffering, having your children killed in wars, and willingness to accept further suffering by future wars. Suffering through education- modern education to achieve a certain technological knowledge and nothing else— that brings great sorrow. So compassion, which is love, can only come when you understand fully the depth of suffering and the ending of suffering. Can that suffering end, not in somebody else, but in you? The Christians have made a parody of suffering—sorry to use that word—but it is actually so. The Hindus have made it into an intellectual affair : what you have done in a past life you are paying for it the present life, and in the future there will be happiness if you behave properly now. But they never behave properly now; so they carry on with this belief which is utterly meaningless. But a man who is serious is concerned with compassion and with what it means to love; because without that you can do what you like, build all the skyscrapers in the world, have marvellous economic conditions and social behaviour, but without it life becomes a desert.

So to understand what it means to live with compassion, you must understand what suffering is. There is suffering from physical pain, physical disease, physical accident, which generally affects the mind, distorts the mind—if you have had physical pain for some time it twists your mind; and to be so aware that the physical pain cannot touch the mind requires tremendous inward awareness. And apart from the physical, there is suffering of every kind, suffering in loneliness, suffering when you are not loved, the longing to be loved and never finding it satisfactory; because we make love into something to be satisfied, we want love to be gratified. There is suffering because of death; suffering because there is never a moment of complete wholeness, a complete sense of totality, but always living in fragmentation, which is contradiction, strife, confusion, misery. And to escape from that we go to temples, and to various forms of entertainment, religious and non-religious, take drugs, group therapy, and individual therapy. You know all those tricks we play upon ourselves and upon others—if you are clever enough to play tricks upon others. So there is this immense suffering brought by man against man. We bring suffering to the animals, we kill them, we eat them, we have destroyed species after species because our love is fragmented. We love God and kill human beings.

Can that end? Can suffering totally end so that there is complete and whole compassion? Because suffering means, the root meaning of that word is to have passion—not the Christian passion, not lust, that is too cheap, easy, but to have compassion, which means passion for all, for all things, and that can only come when there is total freedom from suffering.

You know it is a very complex problem, like fear and pleasure, they are all inter-related. Can one go into it and see whether the mind and the brain can ever be free completely of all psychological suffering, inward suffering. If we don't understand that and are not free of it we will bring suffering to others, as we have done, though you believe in God, in Christ, in Buddha, in all kinds of beliefs—and you have killed men generation after generation. You understand what we do, what our politicians do in India and here. Why is it that human beings who think of themselves as extraordinarily alive and intelligent, why have they allowed themselves to suffer? There is suffering when there is jealousy; jealousy is a form of hate. And envy is part of our structure, part of our nature, which is to compare ourselves with somebody else; and can you live without comparison? We think that without comparison we shall not evolve, we shall not grow, we shall not be some-body. But have you ever tried—really, actually tried—to live without comparing yourself with anybody? You have read the lives of saints and if you are inclined that way, as you get older you want to become like that; not when you are young, you spit on all that. But as you are approaching the grave you wake up.

There are different forms of suffering. Can you look at it, observe it without trying to escape from it?—just remain solidly with that thing. When my wife—I am not married—runs away from me, or looks at another man—by law she belongs to me and I hold her—and when she runs away from me I am jealous; because I possess, and in possession I feel satisfied, I feel safe; and also it is good to be possessed, that also gives satisfaction. And that jealousy, that envy, that hatred, can you look at it without any movement of thought and remain with it? You understand what I am saying? Jealousy is a reaction, a reaction which has been named through memory as jealousy, and I have been educated to run away from it, to rationalise it, or to indulge in it, and hate with anger and all the rest of it. But without doing any of that, can my mind solidly remain with it without any movement? You understand what I am saying? Do it and you will see what happens.

In the same way when you suffer, psychologically, remain with it completely without a single movement of thought. Then you will see out of that suffering comes that strange thing called passion. And if you have no passion of that kind you cannot be creative. Out of that suffering comes compassion. And that energy differs totally from the mechanistic energy of thought.

Chapter 6

DIALOGUE I

"Nobody can put you psychologically into prison. You are already there!"

KRISHNAMURTI: This is in the nature of a dialogue between two friends, talking over their problems, who are concerned not only with their own personal affairs, but also with what is happening in the world. Being serious, these two friends have the urge to transform themselves and see what they can do about the world and all the misery and confusion that is going on. So could we this morning spend some time together having a friendly conversation, not trying to be clever, nor opposing one opinion against another opinion or belief, and together examine earnestly and deeply some of the problems that we have? In this, communication becomes rather important; and any one question is not only personal but universal. So if that is understood, then what shall we talk over together this morning?

Questioner: The compilation of your biography has caused much confusion and quite a lot of questions. I have boiled them down to a few. May I at least hand them over to you.

K: Do you want to discuss the biography written by Mary Lutyens? Do you want to go into that?

Q: No.

K: Thank God! (*laughter*).

Q(I): Briefly and then finish with it.

Q(2): I would propose that you go into the question of correct and incorrect thinking : that is a problem. Both kinds of thought, or thinking processes, are mechanical processes.

K : I see. Can we discuss this? Do you want to talk over the biography—have many of you read it? Some of you. I was just looking at it this morning (*laughter*). Most of it I have forgotten and if you want to talk over some of the questions that have been given me, shall we do that briefly?

Basically the question is : what is the relationship between the present K and the former K? (*laughter*). I should think very little. The basic question is, how was it that the boy who was found there, "discovered" as it was called, how was it that he was not conditioned at all from the beginning, though he was brought up in a very orthodox, traditional Brahmin family with its superstitions, arrogance and extraordinary religious sense of morality and so on? Why wasn't he conditioned *then*? And also later during those periods of the Masters, Initiations and so on—if you have read about it—why wasn't he conditioned? And what is the relationship between that person and the present person? Are you really interested in all this?

Audience: Yes.

K : I am not. The past is dead, buried and gone. I don't know how to tackle this. One of the questions is about the Masters, as they are explained not only in Theosophy but in the Hindu tradition and in the Tibetan tradition, which maintain that there is a Bodhisattva; and that he manifests himself rarely and that is called in Sanskrit Avatar, which means manifestation. This boy was discovered and prepared for that manifestation. And he went through all kinds of things. And one question that may be asked is, must others go through the same process. Christopher Columbus discovered America with sailing boats in dangerous seas and so on, and must we go through all that to go to America? You understand my question? It is much simpler to go by air! That is one question. How that boy was brought up is totally irrelevant; what is relevant is the present teaching and nothing else.

There is a very ancient tradition about the Bodhisattva that there is a state of consciousness, let me put it that way, which is the essence of compassion. And when the world is in chaos that essence of compassion manifests itself. That is the whole idea behind the Avatar and the Bodhisattva. And there are various gradations, initiations, various Masters and so on, and also there is the idea that when he manifests all the others keep quiet. You understand? And that essence of compassion has manifested at other times. What is important in all this, if one may talk about it briefly, is : can the mind passing through all kinds of experiences, either imagined or real—because truth has nothing to do with experience, one cannot possibly experience truth, it is there, you can't experience it—but going through all those various imagined, illusory, or real states, can the mind be left unconditioned? The question is, can the mind be unconditioned always, not only in childhood. I wonder if you understand this question? That is the underlying problem or issue in this.

So as we say, all that is irrelevant. I do not know if you know anything about the ancient tradition of India and Tibet and of China and Japan, about the awakening of certain energy, called Kundalini. There are now all over America, and in Europe, various groups trying to awaken their little energy called Kundalini. You have heard about all this, haven't you? And there are groups practising it. I saw one group on television where a man was teaching them how to awaken Kundalini, that energy, doing all kinds of tricks with all kinds of words and gestures—which all becomes so utterly meaningless and absurd. And there is apparently such an awakening, which I won't go into, because it is much too complex and probably it is not necessary or relevant.

88

So I think I have answered this question, haven't I?

The other question asked was: Is there a non-mechanistic activity? Is there a movement—movement means time—is there a state of mind, which is not only mechanical but not in the field of time? That is what the question raised involves. Do you want to discuss that, or something else? Somebody also sent a written question, "What does it mean to be aware? Is awareness different from attention? Is awareness to be practised systematically or does it come about naturally?" That is the question. Are there any other questions?

Q(1): Would you go into the question of what it means, finding one's true will?

Q(2): What is the difference between denial and suppression?

Q(3): When being together with another person I lose all my awareness; not when I am alone.

K: Can we discuss awareness, begin with that and explore the whole thing, including the will of one's own destiny?

Q: What about earnestness and effort?

K: Earnestness and effort, yes. We are now discussing awareness. Does choice indicate freedom? I choose to belong to this society or to that society, to that cult, to a particular religion or not, I choose a particular job—choice. Does choice indicate freedom? Or does freedom deny choice? Please let us talk this over together.

Q: Freedom means that no choice is needed.

K: But we choose, and we think because we have the capacity to choose that we have freedom. I choose between the Liberal Party and the Communist Party. And in choosing I feel I am free. Or I choose one particular guru or another, and that gives me a feeling that I am free. So does choice lead to awareness?

Q: No.

K : Go slowly.

Q: Choice is the expression of conditioning, is it not?

K : That is what I want to find out.

Q: It seems to me that one either reacts out of habit, or one responds without thinking.

K : We will come to that. We will go into what it means to respond without choice. We are used to choosing; that is our conditioning.

Q: Like and dislike.

K : All that is implied in choice. I chose you as my friend, I deny my friendship to another. One wants to find out if awareness includes choice. Or is awareness a state of mind, a state of observation in which there is no choice whatsoever? Is that possible? One is educated from childhood to choose and that is our tradition, that is our habit, that is our mechanical, instinctive reaction. And we think, because we choose there is freedom. What does awareness mean : to be aware? It implies, doesn't it, not only physical sensitivity, but also sensitivity to the environment, to nature, sensitivity to other people's reactions and to my own reactions. Not, I am sensitive, but to other people I am not sensitive : that is not sensitivity.

So awareness implies, doesn't it, a total sensitivity : to colour, to nature, to all my reactions, how I respond to others, all that is implied in awareness, isn't it? I am aware of this tent, the shape of it and so on. One is aware of nature, the world of nature, the beauty of trees, the silence of the trees, the shape and beauty and the depth and the solitude of trees. And one is aware also of one's relationship to others, intimate and not intimate. In that awareness is there any kind of choice?—in a total awareness, neurologically, physically, psychologically,

to everything around one, the influences, to all the noises and
so on. Is one aware?—not only of one's own beliefs but those
of others, the opinions, judgements, evaluations, the conclusions, all that is implied—otherwise one is not aware. And can
you practise awareness by going to a school or college, or going
to a guru who will teach you how to be aware? Is that awareness? Which means, is sensitivity to be cultivated through
practice?

Q: That becomes selfishness, concentration on oneself.

K : Yes, that is, unless there is total sensitivity, awareness
merely becomes concentration on oneself.

Q: Which excludes awareness.

K : Yes, that is right. But there are so many schools, so many
gurus, so many ashrams, retreats, where this thing is
practised.

Q: When it is practised it is just the old trick again.

K : This is so obvious. One goes to India or Japan to learn
what it means to be aware—Zen practice, all that. Or is
awareness a movement of constant observation? Not only
what I feel, what I think, but what other people say about
me—to listen, if they say it in front of me—and to be aware
of nature, of what is going on in the world. That is total
awareness. Obviously it can't be practised.

Q: It is a non-movement, isn't it?

K : No, it is movement in the sense of, "alive".

Q: It is a participation.

K : Participation implies action. If there is action through
choice, that is one kind of action; if there is an action of
total awareness, that is a totally different kind of action,
obviously. Is one so aware? Or do we indulge in the words,

"being aware"? You understand? To be aware of the people around one, the colour, their attitudes, their walk, the way they eat, the way they think—without indulging in judgement.

Q: Is it something to do with motive? If you have a motive . . .

K : Of course. Motive comes into being when there is choice; that is implied. When I have a motive then choice takes place. I chose you because I like you, or you flatter me, or you give me something or other; another doesn't, therefore there is choice and so on. So is this possible?—this sense of total awareness.

Q: Is there a degree of awareness?

K : That is, is awareness a process of time?

Q: Can one man be more aware than another?

K : Why should I enquire if you are more aware than I am? Just a minute, let us go into it. Why this comparison? Is this not also part of our education, our social conditioning, which says we must compare to progress?—compare one musician with another, one painter with another and so on. And we think by comparing we begin to understand. Comparing means measurement, which implies time, thought, and is it possible to live without comparing at all? You understand? One is brought up, educated in schools, colleges and universities to compare oneself with "A", who is much cleverer than myself, and to try to reach his level—this constant measurement, this constant comparison, and therefore constant imitation, which is mechanical! So can we find out for ourselves whether it is possible to be totally sensitive and therefore aware?

Q: Can you know if you are totally aware or not? Can we be aware of our awareness?

K : No (*laughter*).

Q: You can be aware when you are not aware.

K : Watch it in yourself; verbally it becomes speculative. When you are aware do you know you are aware?

Q: No.

K : Find out. Test it, madam, test it. Do you know when you are happy? The moment you are aware that you are happy it is no longer happiness.

Q: You know when you have got a pain.

K : That is a different matter. When I have pain I am aware of it and I act, do something about it. That is one part of being aware, unless I am paralysed—most people are, in other directions!

So we are asking ourselves, not asking somebody else to tell us, but one is asking oneself if there is that quality of awareness? Does one watch the sky, the evening stars, the moon, the birds, people's reactions, the whole of it? And what is the difference between that awareness and attention? In awareness is there a centre from which you are aware? When I say, "I am aware", then I move from a centre, I respond to nature from a centre, I respond to my friends, to my wife, husband or whatever it is—that centre being my conditioning, my prejudices, my desires, my fears and all the rest of it. In that awareness there is a centre. In attention there is no centre at all. Now please listen to this for two minutes. You are now listening to what is being said and you are giving total attention. That means you are not comparing, you do not say, "I already know what you are going to say", or, "I have read what you have said etc. etc". All that has gone, you are completely attentive and therefore there is no centre and that attention has no border. I don't know if you have noticed?

So, by being aware one discovers that one responds from a centre, from a prejudice, from a conclusion, from a belief, from a conditioning, which is the centre. And from that centre you react, you respond. And when there is an awareness of that centre, that centre yields and in that there is a total attention. I wonder if you understand this? And this you cannot practise; it would be too childish, mechanical. So we go to the next question, which is : "Is there an activity which is not mechanistic?" That means, is there a part of the brain which is non-mechanical. Do you want to go into this? No, no, please, this isn't a game. First of all one has to go into the question of what is a mechanical mind.

Is the brain, which has evolved through millennia, is that totally mechanical? Or is there a part of the brain which is not mechanical, which has never been touched by the machine of evolution? I wonder if you see.

Q: What do you mean by mechanical?

K : We are going to discuss that, sir. Part of this mechanical process is functioning within the field of conditioning. That is, when I act according to a pattern—Catholic, Protestant, Communist, Hindu, whatever it is, a pattern set by society, by my reading, or other influences, and accept that pattern or belief—then that is part of the mechanical process. The other part of the mechanical process is, having had experiences of innumerable kinds which have left memories, to act according to those memories : that is mechanical. Like a computer, which is purely mechanical. Now they are trying to prove it is not so mechanical, but let's leave that alone for the moment.

Mechanical action is accepting tradition and following tradition. One of the aspects of that tradition is acceptance and obedience to a government, to priests. And the mechanical part of the brain is following consciously or unconsciously a line set by thought as the goal and purpose. All that and more is mechanical; and we live that way.

Q: Is thought of itself mechanical?

94

K : Of course, that is the whole point. One has to discover this for oneself, not be told by others, then it becomes mechanical. If we discover for ourselves how mechanical our thinking, our feeling, our attitudes, our opinions are, if one is aware of that, it means thought is invariably mechanistic—thought being the response of memory, experience, knowledge, which is the past. And responding according to the pattern of the past is mechanical, which is thought.

Q: All thought?

K : All thought, of course. Whether noble, ignoble, sexual, or technological thought, it is all thought.

Q: Thought of the great genius also?

K : Absolutely. Wait, we must go into the question of what is a genius. No, we won't go into that yet.

Q: If all thought is mechanical, the expression which you often use, "clear thinking", seems to be a contradiction.

K : No, no. Clear thinking is to see clearly, clear thinking is to think clearly, objectively, sanely, rationally, wholly.

Q: It is still thought.

K : It is still thought, of course it is.

Q: So what is the use of it? (*laughter*).

K : If there was clear thought I wouldn't belong to any political party! I might create a global party—that is another matter.

Q: Can we get back to your question as to whether there is a part of the brain which is untouched by conditioning?

K : That's right, sir; this requires very careful, hesitant, enquiry. Not saying, "Yes, there is", or, "No, there isn't". "I have experienced a state where there is no mechanicalness"—that is too silly. But to really enquire and find out, you need a great deal of subtlety, great attentive quality to go step by step into it, not jump.

So we say most of our lives are mechanical. The pursuit of pleasure is mechanical—but we *are* pursuing pleasure. Now, how shall we find out if there is a part of the brain that is not conditioned? This is a very serious question, it is not for sentimentalists, romantic people, or emotional people; this requires very clear thinking. When you think very clearly you see the limitation of thinking.

Q: Are we going to look very clearly at the barriers which interfere with an unconditioned mind?

K : No, we are trying to understand, or explore together, the mechanical mind first. Without understanding the totality of that you can't find out the other. We have asked the question : "Is there a part of the brain, part of our total mind—in which is included the brain, emotions, neurological responses—which is not completely mechanical?" When I put that question to myself I might imagine that it is not all mechanical because I want the other; therefore I deceive myself. I pretend that I have got the other. So I must completely understand the movement of desire. You follow this? Not suppress it, but understand it, have an insight into it—which means fear, time, and all that we talked about the day before yesterday. So we are now enquiring whether our total activity is mechanistic? That means am I, are you, clinging to memories? The Hitlerian memories and all that, the memories of various pleasurable and painful experiences, the memories of sexual fulfilment and the pleasures and so on. That is : is one living in the past?

Q: Always, I am.

K : Of course! So all that you are is the past, which is mechanical. So knowledge is mechanical. I wonder if you see this?

Q: Why is it so difficult to see this?

K : Because we are not aware of our inward responses, of what actually is going on within ourselves—not to imagine what is going on, or speculate about it, or repeat what we have been told by somebody else, but actually to be aware of what is going on.

Q: Aren't we guided to awareness by experience?

K : No. Now wait a minute. What do you mean by experience? The word itself means, "to go through"—to go through, finish, not retain. You have said something that hurts me, that has left a mark on the brain, and when I meet you that memory responds. Obviously. And is it possible when you hurt me, say something cruel, or justified, or violent, to observe it and not register it? Try it, sir; you try it, test it out.

Q: It is very difficult because the memory has already been hurt; we never forget it.

K : Do go into this. From childhood we are hurt, it happens to everybody, in school, at home, at college, in universities, the whole of society is a process of hurting others. One has been hurt and one lives in that consciously or unconsciously. So there are two problems involved : the past hurt retained in the brain, and not to be hurt; the memory of hurts, and never to be hurt; Now is that possible?

Q: If "you" are not there.

K : Go into it. You will discover it for yourself and find out. That is, you have been hurt.

Q: The image of myself . . .

K : Go into it slowly. What is hurt? The image that you have built about yourself, that has been hurt. Why do you have an image about yourself? Because that is the tradition, part of our education, part of our social reactions. There is an image about myself, and there is an image about you in relation to my image. So I have got half a dozen images and more. And that image about myself has been hurt. You call me a fool and I shrink : it has been hurt. Now, how am I to dissolve that hurt and not be hurt in the future, tomorrow, or the next moment? You follow the question? There are two problems involved in this. One, I have been hurt and that creates a great deal of neurotic activity, resistance, self protection, fear; all that is involved in the past hurt. Second, how not to be hurt any more.

Q: One has to be totally involved.

K : Look at it and you will see. You have been hurt, haven't you—I am not talking to you personally—and you resist, you are afraid of being hurt more. So you build a wall round yourself, isolate yourself, and the extreme form of that isolation is total withdrawal from all relationship. And you remain in that but you have to live, you have to act. So you are always acting from a centre that is hurt and therefore acting neurotically. You can see this happening in the world, in oneself. And how are those hurts to be totally dissolved and not leave a mark? Also in the future how not to be hurt at all? The question is clear, isn't it?

Now how do you approach this question? How to dissolve the hurts, or how not to be hurt at all? Which is the question you put to yourself, which do you want answered? Dissolve all the hurts, or no more hurts? Which is it that comes to you naturally?

Q: No more hurts.

K : So the question is : "Is it possible not to be hurt?" Which means is it possible not to have an image about yourself?

Q: If we see that image is false . . .

K : Not false or true. Don't you see, you are already operating in the field of thought? Is it possible not to have an image at all about yourself, or about another, naturally? And if there is no image, isn't that true freedom? Ah, you don't see it.

Q: Sir, if what happens to you is of no importance to you, then it doesn't matter and it won't hurt you. If you have managed to get rid of your self-importance . . .

K : The gentleman says if you can get rid of your self-importance, your arrogance, your vanity, then you won't be hurt. But how am I to get rid of all that garbage which I have collected? (laughter).

Q: I think you can get rid of it by being entirely aware of the relationship between yourself and your physical body and your thinking. How you control your physical body and . . .

K : I don't want to control anything, my body, my mind, my emotions. That is the traditional, mechanistic response. Sorry! (laughter). Please go into this a little bit and you will see. First of all, the idea of getting rid of an image implies that there is an entity who is different from the image. Therefore he can kick the image. But is the image different from the entity who says, "I must get rid of it"? They are both the same, therefore there is no control. I wonder if you see that. When you see that you are no longer functioning mechanically.

Q: Surely by destroying one image we are immediately building another one?

K : We are going to find out if it is possible to be free of all images, not only the present ones but the future ones. Now why does the mind create an image about itself? I say I am a Christian, that is an image. I believe in the saviour, in Christ, in all the rituals, why? Because that is my conditioning. Go to India and they say, "What are you talking about, Christ? I have got my own gods, as good as yours, if not better" (*laughter*). So that is their conditioning. If I am born in Russia and educated there I say, "I believe in neither. The State is my god and Marx is the first prophet" and so on and so on. So the image formation is brought about through propaganda, conditioning, tradition.

Q: Is that related to the fact that out of fear one behaves in a certain way which is not natural for one to behave; and therefore one is not being oneself? And that is making the image you are talking about.

K: The image is what we call ourself: "I must express myself", "I must fulfil myself". "Myself" is the image according to the environment and culture in which one has been born. I believe there was a tribe in America, among the Red Indians, where anybody who had an image about himself was killed (*laughter*), was liquidated, because it led to ambition and all the rest of it. I wonder what would happen if they did it to all of us. It would be a lovely world, wouldn't it? (*laughter*).

So is it possible not to create images at all? That is, I am aware that I have an image, brought about through culture, through propaganda, tradition, the family, the whole pressure.

Q: We cling to the known.

K: That is the known, tradition is the known. And my mind is afraid to let that known go, to let the image go, because the moment it lets it go it might lose a profitable position in society, might lose status, might lose a certain relationship; so it is frightened and holds on to that image. The image is merely words, it has no reality. It is a series of words, a series of responses to those words, a series of beliefs which are words. I believe in Marx, in Christ, or in Krishna or whatever they believe in in India. They are just words ideologically clothed. And if I am not a slave to words, then I begin to lose the image. I wonder if you see how significant deeply rooted words have become.

Q: If one is listening to what you say and realises that one has an image about oneself, and that there is a large discrepancy between the image one has of oneself and the ideal of freedom . . .

K : It is not an ideal . . .

Q: . . . freedom itself . . . then knowing that there is a discrepancy, can one think of freedom, knowing that it is just an idea?

K : Is freedom an abstraction, a word, or a reality?

Q: It is being free of relationship, is it not?

K : No please, we are jumping from one thing to another. Let us go step by step. We began by asking whether there is any part of the brain, any part of the total entity, that is not conditioned? We said conditioning means image-forming. The image that gets hurt and the image that protects itself from being hurt. And we said there is only freedom—the actuality of that state, not the word, not the abstraction—when there is no image, which is freedom. When I am not a Hindu, Buddhist, Christian, Communist, Socialist, I have no label and therefore no label inside. Now is it possible not to have an image at all? And how does that come about?

Q: Isn't it all to do with the activity . . .

K : Look, we come to a point and go off after something else. One wants to find out whether it is possible to live in this world without a single image.

Q: When there is no observer there is nothing observed, and yet one comes across something in this silence . . .

K : Madam, is this an actual fact that there is no observer in your life—not only occasionally. Is it possible to be free of the image that society, the environment, culture, education has built in one? Because one is all that; you are the result of your environment, of your culture, of your knowledge, of your education, of your job, of your pleasure, you are all that.

Q: What happens to one's sense of orientation without a centre?

K: All that comes a little later, please.

Q: If you are aware of your conditioning does that free you?

K: Now, are you actually aware—not theoretically or in the abstract—actually aware that you are conditioned this way, and therefore you have got an image?

Q: If you don't have the image then you don't know what your place is.

K: "If you have no image then you do not know what your place is." Listen to that carefully. If you have no image, you have no place in the world. Which means if you have no image you are insecure. Go step by step. Now are you, having a place in the world, secure?

Q: No.

K: Be actual.

Q: When you see that the image that you have built, which you are attached to, when you see that it is just a load of words . . .

K: You are finding security in a word: and it is not security at all. We have lived in words and made those words something fantastically real. So if you are seeking security, it is not in an image; it is not in your environment, in your culture. One must have security, that is essential, food, clothes, and shelter; one must have it otherwise one can't function. Now that is denied totally when I belong to a small group. When I say I am a German, or a Russian, or an Englishman, I deny complete security. I deny security because the words, the labels have become important, not security. This is what is actually happening, the Arabs and the Israelis both want security, and both are accepting words and all the rest of it.

Now we come to the point. Is it possible to live in this world, not to go off into some fantastic realm of illusion, or to some monastery, and to live in this world without a single image and be totally secure?

Q: How can we be secure in a sick society?

K: I am going to go into this, madam, I'll show it to you.*

Q: It is competitive, it is vicious.

K: Please go with me. I'll show you that there is complete security, absolute security, not in images.

Q: To be totally aware every moment, then your conditioning does not exist.

K: Not if you are aware. Are you aware that you have an image and that image has been formed by the culture, the society? Are you aware of that image? You discover that image in relationship, don't you? Now we are asking ourselves whether it is possible to be free of images. That means, when you say something to me that is vulgar, hurting, at the moment to be totally aware of what you are saying and how I am responding. Totally aware, not partially, but to be totally aware of both the pleasurable image and the displeasurable image. To be aware totally at the moment of the reaction to your insult or praise. Then at that moment you don't form an image. There is no recording in the brain of the hurt, the insult or the flattery, therefore there is no image. That requires

* See Discussion about security, pages 39–43.

tremendous attention at the moment, which demands a great inward perception, which is only possible when you have looked at it, watched it, when you have *worked*. Don't just say, "Well, tell me all about it; I want to be comfortable".

Q: Who watches all this?

K : Now, who watches all this? If there is a watcher, then the image is continuous. If there is no watcher there is no image. In that state of attention the hurt and the flattery are both observed, not reacted to. You can only observe when there is no observer, who is the past. It is the past observer that gets hurt. Where there is only observation when there is flattery or insult, then it is finished. And that is real freedom.

Now follow it. In this world, if I have no image, you say I shall not be secure. One has found security in things, in a house, in property, in a bank account, that is what we call security. And one has also found security in belief. If I am a Catholic living in Italy, I believe that; it is much safer to believe what ten thousand people believe. There I have a place. And when my belief is questioned I resist.

Now can there be a total awareness of all this? The mind becomes tremendously active, you understand? Not just saying, "I must be aware", "I must learn how to be attentive". You are tremendously active, the brain is alive. Then we can move from that to find out if there is in the brain a part that has not been conditioned at all, a part of the brain which is non-mechanistic. I am putting a false question, I don't know if you see that. Do see it quickly, do see it. Please just listen for two minutes, I am on fire!

If there is no image, which is mechanical, and there is freedom from the image, then there is no part of the brain that has been conditioned. Full stop! Then my whole brain is unconditioned.

Q: It is on fire!

K : Yes, therefore it is non-mechanistic and that has a totally different kind of energy; not the mechanistic energy. I wonder if you see this. Please don't make an abstraction of it because then it becomes words. But to see this, that your brain has been conditioned through centuries, saying survival is only possible if you have an image, which is created by the circle in which you live and that circle gives you complete security. We have accepted that as tradition and we live in that way. I am an Englishman, I am better than anybody else, or a Frenchman, or whatever it is. Now my brain is conditioned, I don't know whether it is the whole or part, I only know that it is conditioned. There can be no enquiry into the unconditioned state until the conditioning is non-existent. So my whole enquiry is to find out whether the mind can be unconditioned, not to jump into the other, because that is too silly. So I am conditioned by belief, by education, by the culture in which I have lived, by everything, and to be totally aware of that, not discard it, not suppress it, not control it, but to be totally aware of it. Then you will find if you have gone that far there is security only in being nothing.

Q: What about images in racial prejudices? Do you belong to a community? I quite agree with you. You don't want any psychological image but you must have a physical image for your physical survival . . . even if you want to drop it everyone forces it on you.

K : Sir, if one wants to survive physically, what is preventing it? All the psychological barriers which man has created. So remove all those psychological barriers and you have complete security.

Q: No, because the other one involves you in it, not yourself.

K : Nobody can put you into prison.

Q: They kill you.

K : Then they kill you, all right (*laughter*). Then you will find out how to meet death (*laughter*). Not imagine what you are going to feel when you die—which is another image. Oh, I don't know if you see all this.

So nobody can put you psychologically into prison. You are already there (*laughter*). We are pointing out that it is possible to be totally free of images, which is the result of our conditioning. And one of the questions about the biography is about that very point. How was that young boy, whatever he was, how was he not conditioned right through? I won't go into that because it is a very complex problem. If one is aware of one's own conditioning then the whole thing becomes very simple. Then genius is something entirely different. And that leaves the question : What is creation?

Chapter 7

DIALOGUE II

"Are you facing in yourself what actually is going on? And can you observe another without the past—without all the accumulated memories, insults, hurts—so that you can look at another with clear eyes?"

Questioner (1): You were going to speak on what is creation; could you say something about creative intelligence?

Q(2): Is there any reality in the belief in reincarnation? And what is the nature and quality of the meditative mind?

Q(3): What is the difference between denial and suppression of habits?

Q(4): You were saying that for the mind to function sanely one must have great security, food and shelter. This seems logical. But it seems that in order to try and find a way to having this security one encounters the horrors and the difficulties which make things so hard and impossible sometimes. What is the right action in this connection?

KRISHNAMURTI: I don't quite follow this.

Q: How are we to live to have this basic security without taking part in all the horrors that are involved in it.

K: You are asking, what is correct action in a world that is chaotic, where there is no security and yet one must have security. What is one to do? Is that the question?

Q(5): I have a question which, when I ask it of myself, I

always come up against a wall. I say, "I am the observer" and I would like to see the whole of the observer. I cannot see the whole of the observer because I can only see in fragments. So how is the observer to see the whole of the observer unless there is no observer? How can the observer see the observer with no observer?

K: How can one see the whole of the observer and can the observer watch himself as the observer. Is that the question?

Q(6): This is about the state of mind in observation. Now when a situation occurs, what holds one to the observation that the observer is not different from what is observed? There seems a lack of attention at the moment, at that point; but that attention requires a tremendous vitality that we don't have.

K: Have I understood the question rightly? We do not have enough energy to observe wholly. Is that it?

Q: Yes.

K: Now which of these questions shall we talk over together?

Q(7): May I ask a question? Can an act of willpower—I think you call it an act of friction—can this generate the vitality or the passion?

K: Can will generate sufficient energy to see clearly? Would that be right?

Q: Yes.

Q(8): What happens to the brain and the process of thought during hypnosis? For medical reasons we use hypnosis. What is the process of thought in that particular case?

K: We have got so many questions. What shall we begin with? The observer?

Q: Yes.

K : To see the whole of the observer one needs energy and how is that energy to be derived? How is that energy to be acquired? And will that energy reveal the totality of the nature and structure of the observer? Should we discuss that? And what is the quality of the mind that has this meditative process? How is one to observe the whole of something, psychologically? How is one to be aware of oneself totally? Can we begin with that?

Q: Surely one can only be aware of the totality if one loses oneself.

K : Yes, sir. Is it possible to see the totality of one's reactions, the motives, the fears, the anxieties, the sorrows, the pain, the totality of all that? Or must one see it in fragments, in layers? Shall we discuss that? How is one to be aware of the content of one's consciousness?

What is consciousness? What do you think is consciousness —under hypnosis, as well as when one is not hypnotised? Most of us are hypnotised—by words, by propaganda, by tradition, by all the things that we believe in. We are hypnotised not only by external influence, but also we have our own peculiar process of hypnotising ourselves into believing something, or not believing and so on. Can one see the totality of one's consciousness? Let us enquire into this.

Q: The observer cannot see it.

K : Don't let us say one can, one cannot, it is so, it is not so. Let's enquire.

Q: One has the feeling one has got to begin!

K : We are going to begin, sir (*laughter*). How shall I begin, from where shall I begin? To be aware of myself, myself being all the beliefs, the dogmas, conclusions, the fears, the anxieties, the pain, the sorrow, the fear of death, the whole of that— where shall we begin to find out the content of this?

Q: You just asked what consciousness was.

K : We are going into that.

Q: If one is going to observe, is it true that one has to stand outside the things that one is observing?

K : Madam, I am asking, if I may, how shall I begin to enquire into the whole structure of myself. If I am interested, if I am serious, where shall I begin?

Q: Is the question, "Who am I?"

K : That becomes intellectual, verbal. I begin to know myself in my relationship to others—do let's face that fact. I cannot know myself in abstraction. Whereas if I could observe what my reactions are in relationship to another, then I begin to enquire. That is much closer, more accurate and revealing. Can we do that? That is, in my relationship to nature, to the neighbour and so on, I discover the nature of myself. So how do I observe my reactions in my relationship with another?

Q: Each time I see something about myself in a reaction it becomes knowledge, it becomes something retainable.

K : I wonder if we are aware what takes place in our relationship with another. You all seem to be so vague about this matter.

Q: When I am very interested in some relationship I notice that I can't really observe. When I am angry in my relationship I see immediately that I really can't observe what is going on.

K : What do we mean by relationship?

Q: When we seem to want something . . .

K : Look at the word first, the meaning of the word.

Q: I like to compare myself with the other person.

K : We are asking the meaning of the word itself, relationship.

Q(1): Communication.

Q(2): It means you are relating to that person.

K : When I say I am related to my wife, or to my husband, father, son, neighbour, what does that mean ?

Q(1): I care for the person.

Q(2): The whole human race is one's brother.

Q(3): I'd rather you told us.

K : Ah! (*laughter*). Relationship means—I am enquiring please, I am not stating it—doesn't relationship mean to respond accurately. To be related, the meaning in the dictionary is, to respond—relationship comes from that word. Now how do I respond in my relationship to you, or to my wife, husband and all the rest of it? Am I responding according to the image I have about you? Or are we both free of the images and therefore responding accurately?

Q: Isn't it largely subconscious?

K : First let us see what the word in itself means.

Q: What do you mean by accurate?

K : Accurate means care—the word accurate means to have great care. If you care for something you act accurately. If you care for your motor you must be very well acquainted with it, you must know all the mechanical processes of it. Accurate means infinite care; we are using that word in that sense. When there is a relationship with another, either intimate, or distant, the response depends on the image you have about the other, or the image the other has about you. And when we act or respond according to that image, it is inaccurate, it is not with complete care.

Q: What is a love and hate relationship?

K : We will come to that. I have an image about you and you have an image about me. That image has been put together through pleasure, fear, nagging, domination, possession, various hurts, impatience and so on. Now when we act or respond according to that image, then that action, being incomplete, is inaccurate, or without care, which we generally call love. Are you aware that you have an image about another? And having that image you respond according to the past, because the image has been put together and has become the past.

Q: And also it is according to one's selfish desires.

K : I said that, fear, desire, selfishness.

Q: You can't think of another person without an image; how can you write a letter without an image?

K : How quickly you want to resolve everything, don't you. First of all, can we be aware that we have an image, not only about ourselves but about another?

Q: The two images are in relation, images of the other are in relation with the image of yourself.

K : You see what you are saying—there is a thing different from the image.

Q: The image of the other is made from the image of yourself.

K : That is what we said.

Q: Would anything practical help?

K : This is the most practical thing if you listen to this. The practical thing is to observe clearly what we are and act from there. Is one aware that one has an image about another? And is one aware that one has an image about oneself? Are you aware of that? This is a simple thing. I injure you, I hurt you, and you naturally have an image about me. I give you pleasure and you have an image about me. And according to that hurt or pleasure you react, and that reaction, being fragmentary, must be inaccurate, not whole. This is simple. Can we go on from there?

Now what do you do with the image you have built about another? I am aware that I have an image about myself and I have an image about you, so I have got two images. Am I conscious of this? Now if I have an image, why has this image been put together? And who is it that has put the image together? You understand the question?

Q(1): Is it fear that creates the image?

Q(2): Is experience a necessary imaginative process?

Q(3): Previous images.

Q(4): Lack of attention.

K: How does it come? Not through lack of something, but how does it come? You say through experience, through various incidents, through words . . .

Q: Retaining it all as memory.

K: Which is all the movement of thought, isn't it? So thought as movement, which is time, put this image together, created this image. It does it because it wants to protect itself. Am I inventing, or fabricating this, or is this actual?

Q: Actual.

K: That means "what is". Actuality means "what is". (Sorry, I am not teaching you English!)

Q: It means that it then can see itself.

K: No, no. You have an image about me, haven't you?

Q: Well, it is changing.

K : Wait, go slow (*laughter*). You have an image about me, haven't you, if you are honest, look into yourself, you see you have an image. How has that image been brought about? You have read something, you have listened to something, there is a reputation, a lot of talk about it, some articles in the papers and so on. So all this has influenced thought and out of that you have created an image. And you have an image, not only about yourself but about the other. So when you respond according to an image about the speaker you are responding inaccurately; in that there is no care. We said care implies attention, affection, accuracy. That means to act according to "what is". Now let's move from there.

Q: Is not an image a thought form?

K : We said that, a thought.

Q: Thought has created images and it seems to imply that thought has created thought so . . .

K : Wait, we will get very far if we go slowly. So thought has built this image through time. It may be one day or fifty years. And I see in my relationship to another this image plays a tremendous part. If I become conscious, if I don't act mechanically, I become aware and see how extraordinarily vital this image is. Then my next question is : is it possible to be free of the image? I have an image as a Communist, believing in all kinds of ideas, or as a Catholic—you follow? This whole cultural economic, social background has built this image also. And I react according to that, there is a reaction according to that image. I think this is clear.

Now is one aware of it? Then one asks : is it necessary? If it is necessary one should keep it, one should have the image. If it is not necessary how is one to be free of it? Now, is it necessary?

Q: Images form the whole chaos in the world where we live, so it is not necessary.

K : He says this whole image-making is bringing about chaos in the world.

Q: Aren't we making a lot of judgements?

K : Are we making a lot of judgements?

Q: In making an image there is a lot of judgement.

K : Yes, but we are asking a little more. We are asking whether it is necessary to have these images?

Q: No, we can be free of it.

K : Is it necessary? First let us see that.

Q: No.

K : Then if it is not necessary why do we keep it? (*laughter*).

Q: I have a feeling, being what we are, we can hardly help it.

K : We are going to find out whether it is possible to be free of this image, and whether it is worth while to be free of this image, and what does it mean to be free of the image.

Q: What is the relation with the chaos? Is it judging that is wrong?

K : No, no, sir. Look, I have an image about myself as a Communist and I believe in Marx, his economic principles, I am strongly committed to that. And I reject everything else. But you think differently and you are committed to that. So there is a division between you and me, and that division invariably brings conflict. I believe that I am Indian and I am committed to Indian nationalism, and you are a committed Muslim and there is division and conflict. So thought has created this division, thought has created these images, these labels, these beliefs and so there is contradiction and division, which brings conflict and therefore chaos. That is a fact. So if you think life is a process of infinite conflicts, never-ending conflicts, then you must keep these images. I don't say it is, we are asking. I believe there have been more than five thousand wars within the last two thousand years and we have accepted that. To have our sons killed because we have these images. And if we see that is not necessary, that it is really a tremendous danger to survival, then I must find out how to be free of the images.

Q: I think something else is involved in this, because you say we always react from the past, but what difference does it make—the past is a cyclic phenomenon that repeats so you can't prevent yourself, you know it is a fact that you will repeat it in the same way all the time.

K : We are talking about the necessity . . .

Q: (*interrupting*) You are pitting yourself against necessity . . .

K : . . . of having an image, or not having an image. If we are clear that these images are a real danger, really a destructive process, then we want to get rid of them. But if you say : I keep my little image and you keep your little image, then we are at each other's throat. So if we can see very clearly that these images, labels, words, are destroying human beings . . .

Q: Krishnamurti, doesn't spiritual commitment give us the penetration or energy? I mean if I am a committed Buddhist and I channel my energy in that direction, it doesn't necessarily mean that I am in conflict with those who aren't Buddhists.

K : Just examine that please. If I am a committed human being, committed to Buddhism, and another is committed to the Christian dogma, and another to Communism . . .

Q: That is not my concern.

K : Isn't this what is happening in life? Don't say it is not my business if you are a Communist. It is my business to see if we can live in security, in peace in the world, we are human beings, supposed to be intelligent. Why should I be committed to anything?

Q: Because it gives energy, the power of penetration.

K : No, no.

Q: The danger is that we are moving away from the central fact.

K : Yes, we are always moving away from the central fact.

Q: We are doing that right now : the image is not necessary.

K : People think it is necessary to be an Englishman, a German, a Hindu, a Catholic, they think it is important. They don't see the danger of it.

Q(1): Some people think it is not necessary.

Q(2): Why don't we see the danger?

K : Because we are so heavily conditioned, it is so profitable. My job depends on it. I might not be able to marry my son to somebody who is a Catholic. All that stuff. So the point is : if one sees the danger of these images, how can the mind free itself from them?

Q: Can "I" be there when no image is formed?

K : Images, whether they are old or new, are the same images.

Q: Yes, but when an image is formed can I be aware?

K : We are first of all going to go into that. How is an image formed? Is it formed through inattention? You get angry with me and if at that moment I am totally attentive to what you say there is no anger. I wonder if you realise this?

Q: So the image and the image-former must be the same in that case.

K : Keep it very simple. I say something that doesn't give you pleasure. You have an image instantly, haven't you? Now at that moment, if you are completely aware, is there an image?

Q: If you don't have that new image, all the other images are gone.

K : Yes, that is the whole point. Can one be attentive at the moment of listening? You are listening now, can you be totally attentive? And when someone calls you by an unpleasant name, or gives you pleasure, at that moment, at that precise moment, can you be totally aware? Have you ever tried this? You can test it out, because that is the only way to find out, not accept the speaker's words. You can test it out. Then if there is no image-forming, and therefore no image, then what is the relationship between the two. You have no image about me, but I have an image about you; then what is your relationship to me? You have no image because you see the danger of it, but I don't see the danger of it, I have my images and you are related to me, as wife, husband, father, whatever it is. I have the image and you have not. Then what is your relationship to me? And what is my relationship to you?

Q: There is a barrier somewhere.

K : Of course there is a barrier, but we are asking what is that relationship. You are my wife; and I am very ambitious, greedy, envious, I want to succeed in this world, make a lot of money, position, prestige, and you say, "How absurd all that is, don't be like that, don't be silly, don't be traditional, don't be mechanical, that is just the old pattern being repeated". What happens between you and me?

Q: Division.

K : And we talk together about love. I go off to the office where I am brutal, ambitious, ruthless, and I come home and am very pleasant to you—because I want to sleep with you. What is the relationship?

Q(1): No good.

Q(2): No relationship.

K: No relationship at all. At last! And yet this is what we call love.

So what is the relationship between you and me when I have an image and you have no image? Either you leave me, or we live in conflict. You don't create conflict but I create conflict because I have an image. So is it possible in our relationship with each other to help each other to be free of images? You understand my question? I am related to you by some misfortune, sexual demands and so on and so on. I am related to you and you are free of the images and I am not, and therefore you care infinitely. I wonder if you see that? To you it is tremendously important to be free of images—and I am your father, wife, husband or whatever it is. Then will you abandon me?

Q: No.

K: Don't say "no" so easily. You care, you have affection, you feel totally differently. So what will you do with me?

Q: There is nothing you can do.

K: Why can't you do something with me? Do go into it, don't theorise about it. You are all in that position. Life is this.

Q(1): It depends if this person has the capacity to see what the truth of the matter is.

Q(2): See through it all and don't take any notice of it (*laughter*).

K: When I am nagging you all the time? You people just play with words. You don't take actuality and look at it.

Q: Surely if you have no image in yourself and you look at another person, you won't see their image either.

K: If I have no image I see very clearly that you have an image. This is happening in the world, this is happening in every family, in every situation in relationship—you have something free and I have not and the battle is between us.

Q: I think that situation is in everything.

K: That is what I am saying. What do you do? Just drop it and disappear and become a monk? Form a community? Go off in meditation and all the rest of it? Here is a tremendous problem.

Q(1): I tell you how I feel, first of all.

Q(2): But surely this is fictitious, because we are trying to imagine.

K: I have said that if you have an image and I have an image, then we live very peacefully because we are both blind and we don't care.

Q: That situation you have created for us because you want us to be free of images!

K: Of course, of course, I want you to be free of images because otherwise we are going to destroy the world.

Q: I see that.

K: The situation is not being created for you: it is there. Look at it.

Q: I have an image about you, and I have had it for a long time. And there are different kinds of images. I have been trying to get rid of those images because I have read that they have created problems for me. Now every time I try to work it out with you; and yet it hasn't helped.

K : I'll show you how to get rid of it, how to be free of images.

Q: I don't believe you, sir.

K : Then don't believe me (*laughter*).

Q: All the time you are just sitting there talking. Abstractions and abstractions. Me having an image about you means you are sitting up on the platform being an enlightened person. I am here as a listener, let's say a disciple or a pupil. Now I feel very strongly that is not actuality or reality because we are two human beings. But still you are the king of gurus, you are the one who knows and ... (*laughter*).

K : Please don't laugh, sirs, be quiet, he is telling you something, please listen. May I show you something?

If that image of the guru has not created a problem you would live with that guru happily, wouldn't you? But it has created a problem, whether it is the guru, the wife, or the husband—it is the same thing. You have got the image about the speaker as the supreme guru (*Krishnamurti and others laugh*)—the word means, one who dispels ignorance, one who dispels the ignorance of another. But generally the gurus impose their ignorance on you. You have an image about me as the guru, or you have an image about another as a Christian and so on. If that pleases you, if that gives you satisfaction you will hold on to it—won't you? That is simple enough. If it causes trouble then you say, "It is terrible to have this" and you move away, form another relationship which is pleasant; but it is the same image-making. So one asks : is it possible to be free of images. The speaker sits on the platform because it is convenient, so you can all see; I can equally sit on the ground but you will have the same image. So the height doesn't make any difference.

The question is, whether the mind—the mind being part of thought, and thought has created these images—can thought dispel these images? Thought has created it and thought can dispel it because it is unsatisfactory and create another image which will be satisfactory. This is what we do. I don't like that guru for various reasons and I go to another because he praises me, gives me garlands and says, "My dear chap, you are the best disciple I have". So thought has created this image. Can thought undo the image?

Q: Not if you are looking at it intellectually. But looking at it intellectually, you are not using your senses.

K : I am asking that first. Look at it. Can the intellect, reasoning, dispel the image?

Q: No.

K : Then what will?

Q: The thing that stands in the way is merely self, the "I". If you overcome this . . .

K : I know; but I don't want to go into the much more complex problem of the "I".

Q: You say the image is what he means by the "I", but what do you mean by the "I"?

K : Of course, of course. How does thought get rid of the image without creating another image?

Q: If the guru causes trouble and it feels uncomfortable with the image, if one can see the trouble then perhaps that guru can help?

K : You are not going into it at all, you are just scratching on the surface.

Q: Thought cannot get rid of the image.

K : If that is so, then what will?

Q: Understanding.

K : Don't use words like understanding. What do you mean by understanding?

Q: Getting rid of the thoughts.

K : Now who is going to get rid of thought?

Q: Is it a question of time? Could it be that our energies are all in the past, and we need to think now?

K : All the images are in the past. Why can't I drop all that and live in the now?

Q: That is what I meant.

K : Yes. How can I? With the burden of the past, how to get rid of the past burden? It comes to the same thing.

Q: If one lives in the present, do the past images still come through?

K : Can you live in the present? Do you know what it means to live in the present? That means not a single memory, except technological memories, not a single breath of the past. Therefore you have to understand the totality of the past, which is all this memory, experience, knowledge, imagination, images. You go from one thing to another, you don't pursue one thing steadily.

Q(1): Please keep going with one having no image and the other having an image.

Q(2): Yes, but we don't answer it.

K : I'll answer it, all right. You have no image and I have an image. What happens? Aren't we eternally at war with each other?

Q: What am I going to do with you?

K : We are living on the same earth, in the same house, meeting often, living in the same community, what will you do with me?

Q: I would try to explain to him what I've learned.

K: Yes, you have explained it to me, but I like my image (*laughter*).

Q: Sir, we cannot know because we have these images of ourselves.

K: That is all I am saying! You are living in images and you don't know how to be free of them. These are all speculative questions.

So let's begin again. Are you aware that you have images? If you have images that are pleasant and you cling to them, and discard those which are unpleasant, you still have images. The question really is, can you be free of them?

Q: Go and listen to some music.

K: The moment that music stops you are back to those images. This is all so childish. Take drugs, that also creates various images.

Q: Isn't there division between wanting to hold on to the images and wanting to let them go.

K: What is the line, the division? The division is desire, isn't it? Listen, sir. I don't like that image, I am going to let it go. But I like this image, I am going to hold on to it. So it is desire, isn't it?

Q: I feel there is a pleasure-motive even in . . .

K: Of course. You don't stick to one thing, sir.

Q: If I have no image, then the other has no image at all.

K: How inaccurate that is. Because I am blind therefore you are also blind! This is so illogical; do think clearly.

What should I do so that there is no image-forming at all? Let us think together.

Q: I think most people—I am sorry—I think most people here are looking for consolation in your words, rather than anything else . . .

K : I am aware that I have images, I know. There is no question of it, I know I have images. I have an image about myself and I have an image about you—that is very clear. If I am satisfied with you and we have the same images, then we are both satisfied. That is, if you think as I think—you like to be ambitious, I like to be ambitious—then we are both in the same boat, we don't quarrel, we accept it, and we live together, work together, are both ruthlessly ambitious. But if you are free of the image of ambition and I am not, the trouble begins. What then will you do, who are free of that image, with me? You can't just say, "Well it is not my business"—because we are living together, we are in the same world, in the same community, in the same group and so on. What will you do with me? Please just listen to this. Will you discard me, will you turn your back on me, will you run away from me, will you join a monastery, learn how to meditate? Do all kinds of things in order to avoid me? Or will you say, "Yes, he is here in my house". What will you do with regard to me, who has an image?

Q: First I would ask you politely to listen.

K : But I won't listen. Haven't you lived with people who are adamant in their beliefs. You are like that.

Q: It is best not to waste one's time.

K : We are going to find out, sir. You see this is really a hypothetical question because you have got images and you live in those images, and the other person lives in images. That is our difficulty. Suppose I have no images, and I haven't, I have worked at this for fifty years, so I have no image about myself, or about you. What is our relationship? I say please listen to me, but you won't. I say please pay attention, which means care, to attend means infinite care. Will you listen to me that way? That means you really want to learn—not from me, but learn about yourself. That means you must infinitely care and watch yourself, not selfishly, but care to learn about yourself —not according to me, or to Freud, or Jung, or to the latest psychologist, but learn about yourself. That means, watch yourself; and you can only do that in your relationship with each other. You say, "You are sitting on that platform and you have gradually assumed, at least in my eyes, a position of authority, you have become my guru". And I say to you, "My friend just listen. I am not your guru. I won't be a guru to anybody." It is monstrous to be a guru. Are you listening when I say this? Or do you say, "I can't listen to you because my mind is wandering". So when you listen, listen with care, with affection, with attention, then you begin to learn about yourself, actually as you are. Then, from there we can move, we can go forward; but if you don't do that, but keep on repeating, "Oh I have got my image, I don't know how to get rid of it" and so on, then we don't move any further.

Now you have an image with regard to sex, that you must have a girl or a boy. We are so conditioned in this. I say to you please listen, are you aware that you are conditioned?— don't choose parts of the conditioning: be totally aware of your whole conditioning. We are conditioned much more at the deeper levels than at the superficial levels—is that clear? One is conditioned very deeply, and superficially less so. Listening with your heart, not with your little mind, with your heart, with the whole of your being, is it possible to be totally aware of all this, the whole of consciousness? To be totally aware implies no observer. The observer is the past and therefore when he observes he brings about fragmentation. When I observe from the past, what I observe brings about a fragmentary outlook. I only see parts, I don't see the whole. This is simple. So I have an insight that says, "Don't look from the past". That means, don't have an observer who is all the time judging, evaluating, saying, "This is right, this is wrong", "I am a Christian, I am a Communist"—all that is the past. Now can you listen to that, which is a fact, which is actual, which is not theoretical? You are facing actually what is. Are you facing in yourself what actually is going on? And can you observe another without the past—without all the accumulated memories, insults, hurts—so that you can look at another with clear eyes? If you say, "I don't know how to do it", then we can go into that.

As we said, any form of authority in this matter is the reaction of submission to somebody who says he knows. That is your image. The professor, the teacher knows mathematics, geography, I don't, so I learn from him, and gradually he becomes my authority. He knows, I don't know. But here, psychologically, I think I don't know how to approach myself, how to learn about it, therefore I look to another—the same process. But the other is equally ignorant as me, because he doesn't know himself. He is tradition-bound, he accepts obedience, he becomes the authority, he says he knows and you don't know: "You become my disciple and I will tell you". The same process. But it is not the same process psychologically. Psychologically the guru is "me". I wonder if you see that? He is as ignorant as myself. He has got a lot of Sanskrit words, a lot of ideas, a lot of superstitions; and I am so gullible I accept him. Here we say there is no authority, no guru, you have to learn about yourself. And to learn about yourself, watch yourself, how you behave with another, how you walk. Then you find that you have an image about yourself, a tremendous image. And you see these images create great harm, they break up the world—the Krishna-conscious group, the Transcendental group, or some other group. And your own group; you have your own ideas, you must have sex, you must have a girl, you must have a boy, and all the rest of it, change the girl, change the boy, every week. You live like that and you don't see the tremendous danger and wastage of life.

Now we come to the point: how am I to be free of all image-making? That is the real question. Is it possible? I will not say it is, or it is not, I am going to find out. I am going to find out by carefully watching why images are made. I realise images are made when the mind is not giving its attention at the moment. At the moment something is said that gives pleasure, or something that brings about displeasure, to be aware at that moment, not afterwards. But we become aware afterwards and say, "My god, I must pay attention, terrible, I see it is important to be attentive and I don't know how to be attentive; I lose it and when the thing takes place it is so quick; and I say to myself I must be attentive". So I beat myself into being attentive—I wonder if you see this— and therefore I am never attentive. So I say to myself, "I am not attentive at the moment something is said which gives pleasure or pain", I see that I am inattentive. I have found that my whole mind, make-up, is inattentive, to the birds, to nature, to everything, I am inattentive—when I walk, when I eat, when I speak, I am inattentive. So I say to myself, "I am not going to be concerned with attention, but pay attention to inattention". Do you get this?

Q: Yes.

K: I am not going to be concerned with being attentive, but I am going to see what is inattention. I am watching inattention, and I see I am inattentive most of the time. So I am going to pay attention to one thing at a time, that is, when I walk, when I eat, I am going to walk, eat, with attention. I am not going to think about something else, but I am going to pay attention to every little thing. So what has been inattention becomes attention. I wonder if you see that?

So I am now watching inattention. That is, I am watching that I am not attentive. I look at a bird and never look at it, my thoughts are all over the place—I am now going to look at that bird; it may take me a second but I am going to look at it. When I walk I am going to watch it. So that out of inattention, without any effort, there is total attention. When there is total attention, then when you say something pleasant or unpleasant there is no image-forming because I am totally there. My whole mind, heart, brain, all the responses are completely awake and attentive. Aren't you very attentive when you are pursuing pleasure? You don't have to talk about attention, you want that pleasure. Sexually, when you want it, you are tremendously attentive, aren't you? Attention implies a mind that is completely awake, which means it doesn't demand challenge. It is only when we have images that challenges come. I wonder if you see this. Because of those images challenges come and you respond to the challenge inadequately. Therefore there is a constant battle between challenge and response, which means the increase of images; and the more it increases the more challenges come, and so there is always the strengthening of images. I wonder if you see this? Haven't you noticed people when they are challenged about their Catholicism or whatever it is, how they become more strong in their opinions? So by being completely attentive there is no image formation, which means conditioning disappears.

Chapter 8

SUFFERING; THE MEANING
OF DEATH

"The mutation in consciousness is the ending of time, which
is the ending of the 'me' which has been produced through
time. Can this take place? Or is it just a theory like any
other?"

MAY WE GO on with what we were discussing the other
day? We were saying that the crisis in the world is not out-
ward but the crisis is in consciousness. And that consciousness
is its content : all the things that man has accumulated through
centuries, his fears, his dogmas, his superstitions, his beliefs, his
conclusions, and all the suffering, pain and anxiety. We said
unless there is a radical mutation in that consciousness, out-
ward activities will bring about more mischief, more sorrow,
more confusion. And to bring about that mutation in consciousness a totally different kind of energy is required; not the
mechanical energy of thought, of time and measure. When we
were investigating into that we said there are three active
principles in human beings : fear, pleasure and suffering. We
talked about fear at some length. And we also went into the
question of pleasure, which is entirely different from joy, enjoyment, and the delight of seeing something beautiful and
so on. And we also touched upon suffering.

I think we ought this morning to go into that question of
suffering. It is a nice morning and I am sorry to go into such
a dark subject. As we said, when there is suffering there can
be no compassion and we asked whether it is at all possible for

human minds, for human beings right throughout the world, to put an end to suffering. For without that ending to suffering we live in darkness, we accept all kinds of beliefs, dogmas, escapes, which bring about much more confusion, more violence and so on. So we are going this morning to investigate together into this question of suffering, whether the human mind can ever be free from it totally; and also we are going to talk about the whole question of death.

Why do we accept suffering, why do we put up with it, psychologically? Physical suffering can be controlled or put up with; and it is important that such physical suffering does not distort clarity of thought. We went into that. Because for most of us, when there is physical pain, a continued suffering, it distorts our thinking, it prevents objective thinking, which becomes personal, broken up, distorted. If one is not actively aware of this whole process of physical suffering, whether remembered in the past, or the fear of having it again in the future, then neurotic habits, neurotic activities take place. We spoke of that briefly the other day.

We are asking if it is at all possible for human beings to end suffering at all levels of their existence, psychological suffering. And when we go into it in ourselves deeply, we see one of the major factors of this suffering is attachment—attachment to ideas, to conclusions, to ideologies, which act as security; and when that security is threatened there is a certain kind of suffering. Please, as we said the other day, we are sharing this together, we are looking into this question of suffering together. You are not merely listening to a talk, if I may point out, and gathering a few ideas and agreeing or disagreeing, but rather we are in communication, sharing the problem, examining the question, the issue, actively; and so it becomes our responsibility, yours as well as the speaker's, to go into this question.

There is also attachment to persons; in our relationships there is a great deal of suffering. That is, the one may be free from this conditioning of fear and so on, and the other may not be and hence there is a tension. The word attachment means "holding on", not only physically but psychologically, depending on something. In a relationship, one may be free and the other may not be free and hence the conflict; one may be a Catholic and the other may not be a Catholic, or a Communist and so on. Hence the conflict that breeds continuous strain and suffering.

Then there is the suffering of the unknown, of death; the suffering of losing something that you were attached to in the past, as memory. I do not know if you have not noticed all these things in yourself? And is it possible to live in complete relationship with another without this tension, which is brought about through self-interest, through self-centred activity, desire pulling in different directions, and live in a relationship in which there may be contradictions, for one may be free, the other may not be? To live in that situation demands not only what is called tolerance—that absurd intellectual thing that man has created—but it demands a much greater thing, which is affection, love, and therefore compassion. We are going to go into that.

We are asking whether man can end suffering. There are various explanations: how to go beyond it, how to rationalise it, how to suppress it, how to escape from it. Now we are asking something entirely different: not to suppress it, not to evade it, nor rationalise it, but when there is that suffering to remain totally with it, without any movement of thought, which is the movement of time and measure.

One suffers: one loses one's son, or wife, or she runs away with somebody else; and the things that you are attached to, the house, the name, the form, all the accumulated conclusions, they seem to fade away, and you suffer. Can one look at that suffering without the observer? We went into that question of what the observer is. We said the observer is the past, the accumulated memory, experience and knowledge.

And with that knowledge, experience, memory, one observes the suffering, so one dissociates oneself from suffering : one is different from suffering and therefore one can do something about it. Whereas the observer *is* the observed.

This requires a little care and attention, the statement that, "the observer is the observed". We don't accept it. We say the observer is entirely different; and the observed is something out there separate from the observer. Now if one looks very closely at that question, at that statement that the observer is the observed, it seems so obvious. When you say you are angry, you are not different from anger, you are that thing which you call anger. When you are jealous, you are that jealousy. The word separates; that is, through the word we recognise the feeling and the recognition is in the past; so we look at that feeling through the word, through the screen of the past, and so separate it. Therefore there is a division between the observer and the observed.

So we are saying that when there is this suffering, either momentary, or a continuous endless series of causes that bring about suffering, to look at it without the observer. You are that suffering; not, you are separate from suffering. Totally remain with that suffering. Then you will notice, if you go that far, if you are willing to observe so closely, that something totally different takes place : a mutation. That is, out of that suffering comes great passion. If you have done it, tested it out, you will find it. It is not the passion of a belief, passion for some cause, passion for some idiotic conclusion. It is totally different from the passion of desire. It is something which is of a totally different kind of energy; not the movement of thought, which is mechanical.

We have a great deal of suffering in what is called love. Love, as we know it now, is pleasure, sexual, the love of a country, the love of an idea, and so on—all derived from pleasure. And when that pleasure is denied there is either hatred, antagonism, or violence. Can there be love, not just something personal between you and me or somebody else, but the enormous feeling of compassion—passion for everything, for everybody. Passion for nature, compassion for the earth on which we live, so that we don't destroy the earth, the animals, the whole thing ... Without love, which is compassion, suffering must continue. And we human beings have put up with it, we accept it as normal. Every religion has tried to find a way out of this, but organised religions have brought tremendous suffering.

Religious organisations throughout the world have done a great deal of harm, there have been religious wars, endless persecution, tortures, burning people, especially in the West— it wasn't the fashion in those days in the East. And we are speaking of—not the acceptance of suffering, or the putting up with suffering—but remaining motionless with that suffering; then there comes out of it great compassion. And from that compassion arises the whole question of creation.

What is creation, what is the creative mind? Is it a mind that suffers and through that suffering has learnt a certain technique and expresses that technique on paper, in marble, with paint—that is, is creativeness the outcome of tension? Is it the outcome of a disordered life? Does creativeness come through the fragmentary activity of daily life? I don't know if you are following all this? Or must we give a totally different kind of meaning to creativeness, which may not need expression at all?

So one has to go into this question within oneself very deeply, because one's consciousness is the consciousness of the world. I do not know if you realise that? Fundamentally your consciousness is the consciousness of the speaker, of the rest of the world, basically. Because in that consciousness there is suffering, there is pain, there is anxiety, there is fear of tomorrow, fear of insecurity, which every man goes through wherever he lives. So your consciousness is the consciousness of the world, and if there is a mutation in that consciousness it affects the total consciousness of human beings. It is a fact. So it becomes tremendously important that human beings bring about a radical transformation, or mutation in themselves, in their consciousness.

Now we can go into this thing called death, which is one of the major factors of suffering. As with everything else in life we want a quick, definite answer, an answer which will be comforting, which will be totally satisfactory, intellectually, emotionally, physically, in every way. We want immortality, whatever that may mean, and we want to survive, both physically and psychologically. We avoid death at any price, put it as far away as possible. So we have never been able to examine it closely. We have never been able to face it, understand it, not only verbally, intellectually, but completely. We wait until the last moment, which may be an accident, disease, old age, when you can't think, when you can't look, you are just "gaga". Then you become a Catholic, a Protestant, believe in this or that. So we are trying this morning to understand, not verbally, but actually what it means to die— which doesn't mean we are asking that we should commit suicide. But we are asking, what is the total significance of this thing called death, which is the ending of what we know as life.

In enquiring into this we must find out whether time has a stop. The stopping of time may be death. It may be the ending and therefore that which ends has a new beginning, not that which has a continuity. So first can there be an ending to time, can time stop?—not chronological time by the watch, as yesterday, today, and tomorrow, the twenty-four hours, but the whole movement of time as thought and measure. That movement, not chronological time, but that movement as thought, which is the whole process of comparing, of measurement, can all that process stop? Can thought, which is the response of memory, and can experience as knowledge— knowledge is always in the past, knowledge is the past

—can that whole momentum come to an end? Not in the technological field, we don't even have to discuss that, that is obvious. Can this movement come to an end? Time as hope, time as something that has happened to which the mind clings, attachment to the past, or a projection from the past to the future as a conclusion, and time as a movement of achievement from alpha to omega—this whole movement in which we are caught. If one said there is no tomorrow, psychologically, you would be shocked, because tomorrow is tremendously important: tomorrow you are going to be happy, tomorrow you will achieve something, tomorrow will be the fulfilment of yesterday's hopes, or today's hopes, and so on. Tomorrow becomes extraordinarily significant—the tomorrow which is projected from the past as thought.

So we are asking, can all that momentum come to an end? Time has created, through centuries, the centre which is the "me". Time is not only the past as attachment, hope, fulfilment, the evolving process of thought until it becomes more and more refined. But also that centre around which all our activities take place, the "me", the mine, we and they, both politically, religiously, economically and so on. So the "me" is the conclusion of time, adding to itself and taking away from itself, but there is always this centre which is the very essence of time. We are asking, can that movement come to an end. This is the whole problem of meditation, not sitting down and repeating some mantra, some words, and doing some tricks—that is all silly nonsense. I am not being intolerant but it is just absurd. And it becomes extraordinarily interesting to find this out, enquire into this.

Then what is death? Can that be answered in terms of words, or must one look at it not only verbally but non-verbally? There is death, the organism dies, by misuse, by abuse, by over-indulgence, drink, drugs, accident, all the things that the flesh is heir to—it dies, comes to an end, the heart stops, the brain with all its marvellous machinery comes to an end. We accept it—we are not afraid of the physical organism coming to an end but we are afraid of something totally different. And being afraid of that basically, we want to resolve that fear through various beliefs, conclusions, hopes.

The whole of the Asiatic world believes in reincarnation; they have proof for it—they say so at least. That is—watch this, it is extraordinary—the thing that has been put together by time as the "me", the ego, that incarnates till that entity becomes perfect and is absorbed into the highest principle, which is Brahman, or whatever you like to call it. Time has created the centre, the "me", the ego, the personality, the character, the tendencies, and so on, and through time you are going to dissolve that very entity, through reincarnation. You see the absurdity? Thought has created something as the "me", the centre, and through the evolutionary process, which is time, you will ultimately dissolve that and be absorbed into the highest principle. And yet they believe in this tremendously. The other day I was talking to somebody who is a great believer in this. He said, "If you don't believe it you are not a religious man", and he walked out. And Christianity has its own form of continuity of the "me", the resurrection—Gabriel blowing the trumpet and so on (*laughter*). When you believe in reincarnation, what is important is that you are going to live another life and you suffer in this life because of your past actions. So what is important is, if one is actually basically committed wholly to that belief, it means that you must behave rightly, accurately, with tremendous care now. And we don't do that. That demands super-human energy.

There are several problems involved in this. What is immortality and what is eternity—which is a timeless state—and what happens to human beings who are still caught in this movement of time? We human beings live extraordinarily complex, irresponsible, ugly, stupid lives, we are at each other's throats, we are battling about beliefs, about authority, politically and religiously, and our daily lives are a series of endless conflicts. And we want that to continue. And because our lives are so empty, so full of meaningless words, we say there is a state where there is no death, immortality—which is a state where there is no movement of time. That is, time through centuries has created the idea of the self, of the "me" evolving. It has been put together through time, which is a part of evolution. And inevitably there is death and with the ending of the brain-cells thought comes to an end. Therefore one hopes that there is something beyond the "me", the super-consciousness, a spark of God, a spark of truth, that can never be destroyed and that continues. And that continuity is what we call immortality. That is what most of us want. If you don't get it through some kind of fame, you want to have it sitting near God, who is timeless. The whole thing is so absurd.

Is there something which is not of time, which has no beginning and no end, and is therefore timeless, eternal? Our life being what it is, we have this problem of death; and if I, a human being, have not totally understood the whole quality of myself, what happens to me when I die? You understand the question? Is that the end of me? I have not understood; if I have understood myself totally, then that is a different problem, which we will come to. If I have not understood myself totally—I am not using the word "understand" intellectually—but actually to be aware of myself without any choice, all the content of my consciousness—if I have not deeply delved into my own structure and the nature of consciousness and I die, what happens?

Now who is going to answer this question? (*laughter*). No, I am putting it purposefully. Who is going to answer this question? Because we think we cannot answer it we look to someone else to tell us, the priest, the books, the people who have said, "I know", the endless mushrooming gurus. If one rejects all authority—and one must, totally, all authority—then what have you left? Then you have the energy to find out—because you have rejected that which dissipates energy,

gurus, hopes and fears, somebody to tell you what happens—if
you reject all that, which means all authority, then you have
tremendous energy. With that energy you can begin to enquire
what actually takes place when you have not totally resolved
the structure and the nature of the self, the self being time,
and therefore movement, and therefore division : the "me"
and the "not me" and hence conflict.

Now what happens to me when I have not ended that conflict? You and I and the rest of the world, if the speaker has
not ended it, what happens to us? We are all going to die—I
hope not soon but sometime or other. What is going to
happen? When we live, as we are living, are we so fundamentally different from somebody else? You may be cleverer,
have greater knowledge or technique, you may be more
learned, have certain gifts, talents, inventiveness; but you and
another are exactly alike basically. Your colour may be different, you may be taller, shorter, but in essence you are the
same. So while you are living you are like the rest of the world,
in the same stream, in the same movement. And when you
die you go on in the same movement. I wonder if you understand what I am saying? It is only the man who is totally
aware of his conditioning, his consciousness, the content of it,
and who moves and dissipates it, who is not in that stream.
Am I making this clear? That is, I am greedy, envious,
ambitious, ruthless, violent—so are you. And that is our daily
life, petty, accepting authority, quarrelling, bitter, not loved
and aching to be loved, the agonies of loneliness, irresponsible
relationship—that is our daily life. And we are like the rest of
the world, it is a vast endless river. And when we die we'll be
like the rest, moving in the same stream as before when we
were living. But the man who understands himself radically,
has resolved all the problems in himself psychologically, he is
not of that stream. He has stepped out of it.

The man who moves away from the stream, his consciousness is entirely different. He is not thinking in terms of time,

continuity, or immortality. But the other man or woman is still in that. So the problem arises: what is the relationship of the man who is out to the man who is in? What is the relationship between truth and reality? Reality being, as we said, all the things that thought has put together. The root meaning of that word reality is, things or thing. And living in the world of things, which is reality, we want to establish a relationship with a world which has no thing—which is impossible.

What we are saying is that consciousness, with all its content, is the movement of time. In that movement all human beings are caught. And even when they die that movement goes on. It is so; this is a fact. And the human being who sees the totality of this—that is the fear, the pleasure and the enormous suffering which man has brought upon himself and created for others, the whole of that, and the nature and the structure of the self, the "me", the total comprehension of that, actually—then he is out of that stream. And that is the crisis in consciousness. We are trying to solve all our human problems, economic, social, political, within the area of that consciousness in time. I wonder if you see this? And therefore we can never solve it. We seem to accept the politican as though he was going to save the world, or the priest, or the analyst, or somebody else. And, as we said, the mutation in consciousness is the ending of time, which is the ending of the "me" which has been produced through time. Can this take place? Or is it just a theory like any other?

Can a human being, can you actually do it? When you do it, it affects the totality of consciousness. Which means in the understanding of oneself, which is the understanding of the world—because I am the world—there comes not only compassion but a totally different kind of energy. This energy, with its compassion, has a totally different kind of action. That action is whole, not fragmentary.

We began by talking about suffering, that the ending of suffering is the beginning of compassion; and this question of love, which man has reduced to mere pleasure; and this great complex problem of death. They are all inter-related, they are not separate. It isn't that I am going to solve the problem of death, forgetting the rest. The whole thing is inter-related, inter-communicated. It is all one. And to see the totality of all that, wholly, is only possible when there is no observer and therefore freedom from all that.

Questioner: I'd like to ask a question. You said towards the beginning that it is important for each individual to transform his consciousness. Isn't the fact that you say that it is important an ideal, which is the very thing to be avoided?

KRISHNAMURTI: When you see a house on fire, isn't it important that you put it out? In that there is no ideal. The house is burning, you are there, and you have to do something about it. But if you are asleep and discussing the colour of the hair of the man who has set the house on fire ...

Q: The house on fire is in the world of reality, isn't it? It is a fact. We are talking about the psychological world.

K: Isn't that also a factual world? Isn't it a fact that you suffer? Isn't it a fact that one is ambitious, greedy, violent— you may not be, but the rest—that is a fact. We say the house is a fact, but my anger, my violence, my stupid activities are something different; they are as real as the house. And if I don't understand myself, dissolve all the misery in myself, the house is going to become the destructive element.

Q: Sir, as I understand it, your message and the message of Jesus Christ seem to reach towards the same thing, although stated differently. I had always understood your message and Jesus Christ's message to be quite different in content. About two years ago I was a Christian, so it is very difficult to get rid of statements that Jesus made, such as, "No man cometh to the Father but by me". Although I find more sense in your message at the moment, how do you equate this?

K: It is very simple. I have no message. I am just pointing out. That is not a message.

Q: But why are you doing it?

K: Why am I doing it? Why do we want a message? Why do we want somebody to give us something? When everything is in you.

Q: It is wonderful.

K: No, it is not wonderful (laughter). Please do look at it. You are the result of all the influences, of the culture, the many words, propaganda, you are that. And if you know how to look, how to read, how to listen, how to see, the art of seeing, everything is there, right in front of you. But we don't have the energy, the inclination, or the interest. We want somebody to tell us what there is on the page. And we make that person who tells us into an extraordinary human being. We worship him, or destroy him, which is the same thing. So it is there. You don't need a message. Do look at it please. Is the book important, or what you find in the book? What you find in the book, and after you have read it you throw it away. Now in these talks, you listen, find out, go into it, and throw away the speaker. The speaker is not at all important. It is like a telephone.

The other question is, "Why do you speak?" Does that need answering? Would you say to the flower on the wayside, "Why do you flower?" It is there for you to look, to listen, to see the beauty of it and come back again to look at the beauty of it. That is all.

Q: (partly inaudible) We have the same message, the same words, we have it in ourselves, the guru.

Q: (repeating) We have a guru in ourselves.

K: Have you? Guru means in Sanskrit, the root meaning of that word means "heavy"

Q: He said heaven.

K: Heaven, it is the same thing, sir. Have you a heaven in yourself? My lord, I wish you had! (*laughter*). In yourself you are so confused, so miserable, so anxious—what a set of words to use—heaven! You can substitute God into heaven, heaven as God and you think you are quite different. People have believed that you had God inside you, light inside you, or something else inside you. But when you see actually that you have nothing, just words, then if there is absolutely nothing there is complete security. And out of that, everything happens, flowers.

Chapter 9

THE SACRED, RELIGION, MEDITATION

"We are going to observe together what is reality, what are the limitations of thought, and whether thought can ever perceive truth. Or is it beyond the realm of thought?

"One must have this meditative quality of the mind, not occasionally, but all day long. And this something that is sacred affects our lives not only during waking hours but during sleep."

I WOULD LIKE this morning to talk about the question of what is sacred, what is the meaning of religion and of meditation. First we must examine what is reality and what is truth. Man has been concerned throughout the ages to discover, or live in truth; And he has projected various symbols, conclusions, images made by the mind or by the hand and imagined what is truth. Or he has tried to find out through the activity and the movement of thought. And I think we should be wise if we would differentiate between reality and truth and when we are clear what reality is then perhaps we shall be able to have an insight into what is truth.

The many religions throughout the world have said that there is an enduring, everlasting truth, but the mere assertion of truth has very little significance. One has to discover it for oneself, not theoretically, intellectually, or sentimentally, but actually find out if one can live in a world that is completely truthful. We mean by religion the gathering together of all energy to investigate into something: to investigate if there is anything sacred. That is the meaning we are giving it, not the religion of belief, dogma, tradition or rituals with their hierarchical outlook. But we are using the word "religion" in the sense: to gather together all energy, which will then be capable of investigating if there is a truth which is not controlled, shaped, or polluted by thought.

The root meaning of the word reality is thing or things. And to go into the question of what is reality, one must understand what thought is. Because our society, our religions, our so-called revelations are essentially the product of thought. It is not my opinion or my judgement, but it is a fact. All religions when you look at them, observe without any prejudice, are the product of thought. That is, you may perceive something, have an insight into truth, and you communicate it verbally to me and I draw from your statement an abstraction and make that into an idea; then I live according to that idea. That is what we have been doing for generations: drawing an abstraction from a statement and living according to that abstraction as a conclusion. And that is generally called religion. So we must find out how limited thought is and what are its capacities, how far it can go, and be totally aware that thought doesn't spill over into a realm in which thought has no place.

I don't know if you can see this? Please, we are not only verbally communicating, which means thinking together, not agreeing or disagreeing, but thinking together, and therefore sharing together; not the speaker gives and you take, but together we are sharing, therefore there is no authority. And also there is a non-verbal communication, which is much more difficult, because unless we see very clearly the full meaning of words, how the mind is caught in words, how words shape our thinking, and can go beyond that, then there is no non-verbal communication, which becomes much more significant. We are trying to do both: to communicate verbally and non-verbally. That means we must both be interested at the same time, at the same level, with the same intensity, otherwise we shan't communicate. It is like love; love is that intense feeling at the same time, at the same level. Otherwise you and I don't love each other. So we are going to observe together what is reality, what are the limitations of thought, and whether thought can ever perceive truth. Or is it beyond the realm of thought?

I think we all agree, at least most of us do, even the scientists, that thought is a material process, is a chemical process. Thought is the response of accumulated knowledge as experience and memory. So thought is essentially a thing. There is no sacred thought, no noble thought, it is a thing. And its function is in the world of things, which is technology, learning, learning the art of learning, the art of seeing and listening. And reality is in that area. Unless we understand this rather complex problem we shall not be able to go beyond it. We may pretend, or imagine, but imagination and pretension have no place in a human being who is really serious and is desirous to find out what is truth.

As long as there is the movement of thought, which is time and measure, in that area truth has no place. Reality is that which we think and the action of thought as an idea, as a principle, as an ideal, projected from the previous knowledge into the future modified and so on. All that is in the world of reality. We live in that world of reality—if you have observed yourself you will see how memory plays an immense part. Memory is mechanical, thought is mechanical, it is a form of computer, a machine, as the brain is. And thought has its place. I cannot speak if I have no language; if I spoke in Greek you wouldn't understand. And learning a language, learning to drive a car, to work in a factory and so on, there thought is necessary. Psychologically, thought has created the reality of the "me". "Me", "my", my house, my property, my wife, my husband, my children, my country, my God—all that is the product of thought. And in that field we have established a relationship with each other which is constantly in conflict. That is the limitation of thought.

Unless we put order into that world of reality we cannot go further. We live a disorderly life in our daily activities; that is a fact. And is it possible to bring about order in the world of reality, in the world of thought, socially, morally, ethically and so on? And who is to bring about order in the world of reality? I live a disorderly life—if I do—and being disorderly, can I bring about order in all the activities of daily life? Our daily life is based on thought, our relationship is based on thought, because I have an image of you and you have an image of me, and the relationship is between those two images. The images are the product of thought, which is the response of memory, experience and so on. Now can there be order in the world of reality? This is really a very important question. Unless order is established in the world of reality there is no foundation for further enquiry. In the world of reality, is it possible to behave orderly, not according to a pattern set by thought, which is still disorder? Is it possible to bring about order in the world of reality? That is, no wars, no conflict, no division. Order implies great virtue, virtue is the essence of order—not following a blueprint, which becomes mechanical. So who is to bring order in this world of reality? Man has said, "God will bring it. Believe in God and you will have order. Love God and you will have order." But this order becomes mechanical because our desire is to be secure, to survive, to find the easiest way of living—let us put it that way.

So we are asking, who is to bring order in this world of reality, where there is such confusion, misery, pain, violence and so on. Can thought bring about order in that reality—a world of reality which thought has created? Do you follow my question? The Communists say control the environment, then there will be order in man. According to Marx the State will wither away—you know all that. They have tried to bring order but man is in disorder, even in Russia! So one has to find out, if thought is not to bring about order, then what will? I don't know if this is a problem to you, if it really interests you? So one has to ask, if thought, which has made such a mess of life, cannot bring clarity into this world of reality, then is there an observation in the field of reality, or of the field of reality, without the movement of thought. Are we meeting each other about this? A human being has exercised thought; he says there is disorder, I will control it, I will shape it, I will make order according to certain ideas—it is all the product of thought. And thought has created disorder. So thought has no place in order, and how is this order to come about?

Now we will go into it a little bit. Can one observe this disorder in which one lives, which is conflict, contradiction, opposing desires, pain, suffering, fear, pleasure and all that, this whole structure of disorder, without thought? You understand my question? Can you observe this enormous disorder in which we live, externally as well as inwardly, without any movement of thought? Because if there is any movement of thought, then it is going to create further disorder, isn't it? So can you observe this disorder in yourself without any movement of thought as time and measure—that is, without any movement of memory?

We are going to see whether thought as time can come to an end. Whether thought as measure, which is comparison, as time, from here to there—all that is involved in the movement of time—whether that time can have a stop? This is the very essence of meditation. You understand? So we are going to enquire together if time has a stop, that is, if thought as movement can come to an end. Then only is there order and therefore virtue. Not cultivated virtue, which requires time and is therefore not virtue, but the very stopping, the very ending of thought *is* virtue. This means we have to enquire into the whole question of what is freedom. Can man live in freedom? Because that is what it comes to. If time comes to an end it means that man is deeply free. So one has to go into this question of what is freedom. Is freedom relative, or absolute? If freedom is the outcome of thought then it is relative. When freedom is not bound by thought then it is absolute. We are going to go into that.

Outwardly, politically, there is less and less freedom. We think politicians can solve all our problems and the politicians, especially the tyrannical politicians, assume the authority of God, they know and you don't know. That is what is going on in India, freedom of speech, civil rights, have been denied, like in all tyrannies. Democratically we have freedom of choice, we choose between the Liberals, Conservatives, Labour or something else. And we think that having the capacity to choose gives us freedom. Choice is the very denial of freedom. You choose when you are not clear, when there is no direct perception, and so you choose out of confusion, and so there is no freedom in choice—psychologically, that is. I can choose between this cloth and that cloth, and so on; but psychologically we think we are free when we have the capacity to choose. And we are saying that choice is born out of confusion, out of the structure of thought, and therefore it is not free. We accept the authority of the gurus, the priests, because we think they know and we don't know. Now if you examine the whole idea of the guru, which is becoming rather a nuisance in this country and in America, the world over—I am sorry I am rather allergic to gurus (*laughter*), I know many of them, they come to see me (*laughter*). They say, "What you are saying is the highest truth"—they know how to flatter! But we are dealing, they say, with people who are ignorant and we are the intermediaries: we want to help them. So they assume the authority and therefore deny freedom. I do not know if you have noticed that not one single guru has raised his voice against tyranny.

A man who would understand what freedom is must totally deny authority, which is extraordinarily difficult, it demands great attention. We may reject the authority of a guru, of a priest, of an idea, but we establish an authority in ourselves—that is "I think it is right, I know what I am saying, it is my experience". All that gives one the authority to assert, which is the same thing as the guru and the priest.

Can the mind be free of authority, of tradition, which means accepting another as your guide, as somebody to tell you what to do, except in the technological field? And man must be free if he is not to become a serf, a slave, and deny the beauty and depth of the human spirit. Now can the mind put aside all authority in the psychological sense?—if you put aside the authority of the policeman you will be in trouble. That requires a great deal of inward awareness. One obeys and accepts authority because in oneself there is uncertainty, confusion, loneliness, and the desire to find something permanent, something lasting. And is there anything lasting, anything that is permanent, created by thought? Or does thought give to itself permanency? The mind desires to have something it can cling to, some certainty, some psychological security. This is what happens in all our relationships with each other. I depend on you psychologically—because in myself I am uncertain, confused, lonely—and I am attached to you, I possess you, I dominate you. So living in this world is freedom possible, without authority, without the image, without the sense of dependency? And is it freedom *from* something or freedom *per se*?

Now can we have freedom in the world of reality? You understand my question?—can there be freedom in my relationship with you? Can there be freedom in relationship between man and woman, or is that impossible?—which doesn't mean freedom to do what one likes, or permissiveness, or promiscuity. But can there be a relationship between human beings of complete freedom? I do not know if you have ever asked this question of yourself? You might say it is possible or not possible. The possibility or the impossibility of it is not an answer, but to find out whether freedom can exist, absolute freedom in our relationships. That freedom can only exist in relationship when there is order : order not according to you, or another, but order in the sense of the observation of disorder. And that observation is not the movement of thought, because the observer is the observed; only then there is freedom in our relationship.

Then we can go to something else. Having observed the whole nature of disorder, order comes into being in our life. That is a fact, if you have gone into it. From there we can move and find out whether thought can end, can realise its own movement, see its own limitation and therefore stop. We are asking, what place has time in freedom. Is freedom a state of mind in which there is no time?—time being movement of thought as time and measure. Thought is movement, movement in time. That is, can the brain, which is part of the mind —which has evolved through centuries with all the accumulated memories, knowledge, experience—is there a part of the brain which is not touched by time? Do you understand my question? Our brain is conditioned by various influences, by the pursuit of desires; and is there a part of the brain that is not conditioned at all? Or is the whole brain conditioned and can human beings therefore never escape from conditioning? They can modify the conditioning, polish, refine it, but there will always be conditioning if the totality of the brain is limited, and therefore no freedom.

So we are going to find out if there is any part of the brain that is not conditioned. All this is meditation, to find out. Can one be aware of the conditioning in which one lives? Can you be aware of your conditioning as a Christian, a Capitalist, a Socialist, a Liberal, that you believe in this and you don't believe in that?—all that is part of the conditioning. Can a human being be aware of that conditioning? Can you be aware of your consciousness?—not as an observer, but that you *are* that consciousness. And if you are aware, who is it that is aware? Is it thought that is aware that it is conditioned?

Then it is still in the field of reality, which is conditioned. Or is there an observation, an awareness in which there is pure observation? Is there an act, or an art of pure listening?

Do listen to this a little bit. The word "art" means to put everything in its right place, where it belongs. Now can you observe without any interpretation, without any judgement, without any prejudice—just observe, see purely? And also can you listen, as you are doing now, without any movement of thought. It is only possible if you put thought in the right place. And the art of learning means not accumulating—then it becomes knowledge and thought—but the movement of learning, without the accumulation. So there is the art of seeing, the art of listening, the art of learning—which means to put everything where it belongs. And in that there is great order.

Now we are going to find out if time has a stop. This is meditation. As we said at the beginning, it is all in the field of meditation. Meditation isn't something separate from life, from daily life. Meditation is not the repetition of words, the repetition of a mantra, which is now the fashion and called transcendental meditation, or the meditation which can be practised. Meditation must be something totally unconscious. I wonder if you see this? If you practise meditation, that is follow a system, a method, then it is the movement of thought, put together in order to achieve a result, and that result is projected as a reaction from the past and therefore still within the area of thought.

So can there be a mutation in the brain? It comes to that. We say it is possible. That is, a mutation is only possible when there is a great shock of attention. Attention implies no control. Have you ever asked whether you can live in this world without a single control?—of your desires, of your appetites, of the fulfilment of your desires and so on, without a single breath of control? Control implies a controller : and the controller thinks he is different from that which he controls. But when you observe closely the controller is the controlled. So what place has control? In the sense of restraint, suppression, to control in order to achieve, to control to change yourself to become something else—all that is the demand of thought. Thought by its very nature being fragmentary, divides the controller and the controlled. And we are educated from childhood to control, to suppress, to inhibit—which does not mean to do what you like; that is impossible, that is too absurd, too immature. But to understand this whole question of control demands that you examine the desire which brings about this fragmentation; the desire to be and not to be. To find out whether you can live without comparison, therefore without an ideal, without a future—all that is implied in comparison. And where there is comparison there must be control. Can you live without comparison and therefore without control—do you understand? Have you ever tried to live without control, without comparison? Because comparison and control are highly respectable. The word "respect" means to look about. And when we look about we see that all human beings, wherever they live, have this extraordinary desire to compare themselves with somebody, or with an idea, or with some human being who is supposed to be noble, and in that process they control, suppress. Now if you see this whole movement, then one will live without a single breath of control. That requires tremendous inward discipline. Discipline means actually to learn, not to be disciplined to a pattern like a soldier. The word "discipline" means to learn. Learn whether it is possible to live without a single choice, comparison, or control. To learn about it; not to accept it, not to deny it, but to find out how to live.

Then out of that comes a brain which is not conditioned. Meditation then is freedom from authority, putting everything in its right place in the field of reality, and consciousness realising its own limitation and therefore bringing about order in that limitation. When there is order there is virtue, virtue in behaviour.

From there we can go into the question, whether time has a stop. Which means, can the mind, the brain itself, be absolutely still?—not controlled. If you control thought in order to be still, then it is still the movement of thought. Can the brain and the mind be absolutely still, which is the ending of time? Man has always desired throughout the ages to bring silence to the mind, which he calls meditation, contemplation and so on. Can the mind be still?—not chattering, not imagining, not conscious of that stillness, because if you are conscious of that stillness there is a centre which is conscious, and that centre is part of time, put together by thought; therefore you are still within the area of reality and there is no ending in the world of reality of time.

Man has made, whether by the hand or by the mind, what he thinks is sacred, all the images in churches, in temples. All those images are still the product of thought. And in that there is nothing sacred. But out of this complete silence is there anything sacred? We began by saying that religion is not belief, rituals, authority, but religion is the gathering of all energy to investigate if there is something sacred which is not the product of thought. We have that energy when there is complete order in the world of reality in which we live—order in relationship, freedom from authority, freedom from comparison, control, measurement. Then the mind and the brain become completely still naturally, not through compulsion. If one sees that anything which thought has created is not sacred, nothing—all the churches, all the temples, all the mosques in the world have no truth—then is there anything sacred?

In India, when only Brahmins could enter Temples and Ghandi was saying that all people can enter temples—I followed him around one year—and I was asked, "What do you say to that"? I replied, God is not in temples, it doesn't matter who enters. That was of course not acceptable. So in the same way we are saying that anything created by thought is not sacred, and is there anything sacred? Unless human beings find that sacredness, their life really has no meaning, it is an empty shell. They may be very orderly, they may be relatively free, but unless there is this thing that is totally sacred, untouched by thought, life has no deep meaning. Is there something sacred, or is everything matter, everything thought, everything transient, everything impermanent? Is there something that thought can never touch and therefore is incorruptible, timeless, eternal and sacred? To come upon this the mind must be completely, totally still, which means time comes to an end; and in that there must be complete freedom from all prejudice, opinion, judgement—you follow? Then only one comes upon this extraordinary thing that is timeless and the very essence of compassion.

So meditation has significance. One must have this meditative quality of the mind, not occasionally, but all day long. And this something that is sacred affects our lives not only during the waking hours but during sleep. And in this process of meditation there are all kinds of powers that come into being: one becomes clairvoyant, the body becomes extraordinarily sensitive. Now clairvoyance, healing, thought transference and so on, become totally unimportant; all the occult powers become so utterly irrelevant, and when you pursue those you are pursuing something that will ultimately lead to illusion. That is one factor. Then there is the factor of sleep. What is the importance of sleep? Is it to spend the sleeping hours dreaming? Or is it possible not to dream at all? What are dreams, why do we dream, and is it possible for a mind not to dream, so that during sleep, the mind being utterly restful, a totally different kind of energy is built in?

If during waking hours we are completely attentive to our thoughts, to our actions, to our behaviour, totally aware, then are dreams necessary? Or are dreams a continuation of our daily life, in the form of pictures, images, incidents—a continuity of our daily conscious or unconscious movements? So when the mind becomes totally aware during the day, then you will see that dreams become unimportant, and being unimportant they have no significance and therefore there is no dreaming. There is only complete sleep; that means the mind has complete rest: it can renew itself. Test it out. If you accept what the speaker is saying, then it is futile; but not if you enquire and find out if during the day you are very very awake, watchful, aware without choice—we went into what it is to be aware—then out of that awareness when you do sleep, the mind becomes extraordinarily fresh and young. Youth is the essence of decision, action. And if that action is merely centred round itself, round the centre of myself, then that action breeds mischief, confusion and so on. But when you realise the whole movement of life as one, undivided, and are aware of that, then the mind rejuvenates itself and has immense energy. All that is part of meditation.

PART III

Some Questions and Answers

Chapter 10

RIGHT LIVELIHOOD

Questioner: Is a motive necessary in business? What is the right motive in earning a livelihood?

KRISHNAMURTI: What do you think is the right livelihood?—not what is the most convenient, not what is the most profitable, enjoyable, or gainful; but what is the right livelihood? Now, how will you find out what is right? The word "right" means correct, accurate. It cannot be accurate if you do something for profit or pleasure. This is a complex thing. Everything that thought has put together is reality. This tent has been put together by thought, it is a reality. The tree has not been put together by thought, but it is a reality. Illusions are reality—the illusions that one has, imagination, all that is reality. And the action from those illusions is neurotic, which is also reality. So when you ask this question, "What is the right livelihood", you must understand what reality is. Reality is not truth.

Now what is correct action in this reality? And how will you discover what is right in this reality?—discover for yourself, not be told. So we have to find out what is the accurate, correct, right action, or right livelihood in the world of reality, and reality includes illusion. Don't escape, don't move away; belief is an illusion, and the activities of belief are neurotic; nationalism and all the rest of it is another form of reality, but an illusion. So taking all that as reality, what is the right action there?

Who is going to tell you? Nobody, obviously. But when you

see reality without illusion, the very perception of that reality is your intelligence, isn't it? in which there is no mixture of reality and illusion. So when there is observation of reality, the reality of the tree, the reality of the tent, reality which thought has put together, including visions, illusions, when you see all that reality, the very perception of that is your intelligence— isn't it? So your intelligence says what you are going to do. I wonder if you understand this? Intelligence is to perceive what is and what is not—to perceive "what is" and see the reality of "what is", which means you don't have any psychological involvement, any psychological demands, which are all forms of illusion. To see all that is intelligence; and that intelligence will operate wherever you are. Therefore that will tell you what to do.

Then what is truth? What is the link between reality and truth? The link is this intelligence. Intelligence that sees the totality of reality and therefore doesn't carry it over to truth. And the truth then operates on reality through intelligence.

Chapter 11

WILL

Questioner: I wish to know if effort of will has a place in life.

KRISHNAMURTI: Has the will a place in life? What do we mean by life?—going to the office every day, having a profession, a career, the everlasting climbing the ladder, both religiously and mundanely, the fears, the agonies, the things that we have treasured, remembered, all that is life, isn't it? All that is life, both the conscious as well as the hidden. The conscious of which we know, more or less; and all the deep down hidden things in the cave of one's mind, in the deepest recesses of one's mind. All that is life: the illusion and the reality, the highest principle and the "what is", the fear of death, fear of living, fear of relationship—all that. What place has will in that? That is the question.

I say it has no place. Don't accept what I am saying; I am not your authority, I am not your guru. All the content of one's consciousness, which *is* consciousness, is created by thought, which is desire and image. And that is what has brought about such havoc in the world. Is there a way of living in this world without the action of will? That is the present question.

I know this, as a human being I am fully aware of what is going on within my consciousness, the confusion, the disorder, the chaos, the battle, the seeking for power, position, safety, security, prominence, all that; and I see thought has created all that. Thought plus desire and the multiplication of images. And I say, "What place has will in this?" It is will that has created this. Now can I live in this without will? Biologically, physiologically, I have to exercise a certain form of energy to learn a language, to do this and that. There must be a certain drive. I see all this. And I realise—not as a verbal realisation, as a description, but the actual fact of it, as one realises pain in the body—I realise that this is the product of thought as desire and will. Can I, as a human being, look at all this, and transform this without will?

Now what becomes important is what kind of observation is necessary. Observation to see actually what is. Is the mind capable of seeing actually "what is"? Or does it always translate into "what should be", "what should not be", "I must suppress", "I must not suppress", and all the rest of it? There must be freedom to observe, otherwise I can't see. If I am prejudiced against you, or like you, I can't see you. So freedom is absolutely necessary to observe—freedom from prejudice, from information, from what has been learned, to be able to look without the idea. You understand: to look without the idea. As we said the other day, the word "idea" comes from Greek; the root meaning of that word is to observe, to see. When we refuse to see, we make an abstraction and make it into an idea.

There must be freedom to observe, and in that freedom will is not necessary; there is just freedom to look. Which means, to put it differently, if one makes a statement, can you listen to it without making it into an abstraction? Do you understand my question? The speaker makes a statement such as, "The ending of sorrow is the beginning of wisdom". Can you listen to that statement without making an abstraction of it?—the abstraction being: "Is that possible?", "What do we get from it?", "How do we do it?". Those are all abstractions—and not actually listening. So can you listen to that statement with all your senses, which means with all your attention? Then you see the truth of it. And the perception of that truth is action in this chaos.

Chapter 12

EMOTIONS AND THOUGHT

Questioner: Are emotions rooted in thought?

KRISHNAMURTI: What are emotions? Emotions are sensations, aren't they? You see a lovely car, or a beautiful house, a beautiful woman or man, and the sensory perception awakens the senses. Then what takes place? Contact, then desire, Now thought comes in. Can you end there and not let thought come in and take over? I see a beautiful house, the right proportions, with a lovely lawn, a nice garden: all the senses are responding because there is great beauty—it is well kept, orderly, tidy. Why can't you stop there and not let thought come in and say, "I must have" and all the rest of it? Then you will see emotions, or sensations, are natural, healthy, normal. But when thought takes over, then all the mischief begins.

So to find out for oneself whether it is possible to look at something with all the senses and end there and not proceed further—do it! That requires an extraordinary sense of awareness in which there is no control; no control, therefore no conflict. Just to observe totally that which is, and all the senses respond and end there. There is great beauty in that. For after all what is beauty?

Chapter 13

BEAUTY

IS BEAUTY IN the world of reality? Or is it not within the movement of thought as time? Please follow this carefully because we are investigating together. I am not laying down the law. I am just asking myself : does beauty lie within the movement of thought as time? That is, within the field of reality. There are beautiful paintings, statues, sculpture, marvellous cathedrals, wonderful temples. If you have been to India, some of those ancient temples are really quite extraordinary : they have no time, there has been no entity as a human being who put them together. And those marvellous old sculptures from the Egyptians, from the Greeks, down to the Moderns. That is, is it expression *and* creation? Does creation need expression? I am not saying it does, or does not, I am asking, enquiring. Is beauty, which is both expression outwardly and the sense of inward feeling of extraordinary elation, that which comes when there is complete cessation of the "me", with all its movements?

To enquire what is beauty, we have to go into the question of what is creation. What is the mind that is creative? Can the mind that is fragmented, however capable, whatever its gifts, talent, is such a mind creative? If I live a fragmented life, pursuing my cravings, my selfishness, my self-centred ambitions, pursuits, my pain, my struggle—is such a mind (I am asking) creative?—though it has produced marvellous music, marvellous literature, architecture and poetry—English and other literature is filled with it. A mind that is not whole, can that be creative? Or is creation only possible when there is total wholeness and therefore no fragmentation? A mind that is fragmented is not a beautiful mind, and therefore it is not creative.

Chapter 14

THE STREAM OF "SELFISHNESS"

ONE CAN SEE that thought has built the "me", the "me" that has become independent, the "me" that has acquired knowledge, the "me" that is the observer, the "me" that is the past and which passes through the present and modifies itself as the future. It is still the "me" put together by thought, and that "me" has become independent of thought. That "me" has a name, a form. It has a label called X or Y or John. It identifies with the body, with the face; there is the identification of the "me" with the name and with the form, which is the structure, and with the ideal which it wants to pursue. Also with the desire to change the "me" into another form of "me", with another name. This "me" is the produce of time and of thought. The "me" is the word: remove the word and what is the "me"?

And that "me" suffers: the "me", as you, suffers. The "me" in suffering is you. The "me" in its great anxiety is the great anxiety of you. Therefore you and I are common; that is the basic essence. Though you may be taller, shorter, have a different temperament, different character, be cleverer, all that is the peripheral field of culture; but deep down, basically we are the same. So that "me" is moving in the stream of greed, in the stream of selfishness, in the stream of fear, anxiety and so on, which is the same as you in the stream. Please don't accept what I am saying—see the truth of it. That is, you are selfish and another is selfish; you are frightened, another is frightened; you are aching, suffering, with tears, greed, envy, that is the common lot of all human beings. That is the stream in which we are living, the stream in which we are caught, all of us. We are caught in that stream while we are living; please see that we are caught in this stream as an act of life. This stream is "selfishness"—let us put it that way—and in this stream we are living—the stream of "selfishness"—that expression includes all the descriptions of the "me" which I have just now given. And when we die the organism dies, but the selfish stream goes on. Just look at it, consider it.

Suppose I have lived a very selfish life, in self-centred activity, with my desires, the importance of my desires, ambitions, greed, envy, the accumulation of property, the accumulation of knowledge, the accumulation of all kinds of things which I have gathered—all of which I have termed as "selfishness". And that is the thing I live in, that is the "me", and that is you also. In our relationships it is the same. So while living we are together flowing in the stream of selfishness. This is a fact, not my opinion, not my conclusion; if you observe you will see it, whether you go to America, to India, or all over Europe, modified by the environmental pressures and so on, but basically that is the movement. And when the body dies that movement goes on . . . That stream is time. That is the movement of thought, which has created suffering, which has created the "me" from which the "me" has now asserted itself as being independent, dividing itself from you; but the "me" is the same as you when it suffers. The "me" is the imagined structure of thought. In itself it has no reality. It is what thought has made it because thought needs security, certainty, so it has invested in the "me" all its certainty. And in that there is suffering. In that movement of selfishness, while we are living we are being carried in that stream and when we die that stream exists.

Is it possible for that stream to end? Can selfishness, with all its decorations, with all its subtleties, come totally to an end? And the ending is the ending of time. Therefore there is a totally different manifestation after the ending, which is: no selfishness at all.

When there is suffering, is there a "you" and "me"? Or is there only suffering? I identify myself as the "me" in that suffering, which is the process of thought. But the actual fact is you suffer and I suffer, not "I" suffer something independent of you, who are suffering. So there is only suffering . . . there is only the factor of suffering. Do you know what it does when you realise that? Out of that non-personalised suffering, not identified as the "me" separate from you, when there is that suffering, out of that comes a tremendous sense of compassion. The very word "suffering" comes from the word "passion".

So I have got this problem. As a human being, living, knowing that I exist in the stream as selfishness, can that stream, can that movement of time, come totally to an end? Both at the conscious as well as at the deep level? Do you understand my question, after describing all this? Now, how will you find out whether you, who are caught in that stream of selfishness, can completely step out of it?—which is the ending of time. Death is the ending of time as the movement of thought if there is the stepping out of that. Can you, living in this world, with all the beastliness of it, the world that man has made, that thought has made, the dictatorships, the totalitarian authority, the destruction of human minds, destruction of the earth, the animals, everything man touches he destroys, including his wife or husband. Now can you live in this world completely without time?—that means no longer caught in that stream of selfishness?

You see there are many more things involved in this; because there is such a thing as great mystery. Not the thing invented by thought, that is not mysterious. The occult is not mysterious, which everybody is chasing now, that is the fashion. The experiences which drugs give are not mysterious.

There is this thing called death, and the mystery that lies where there is a possibility of stepping out of it.

That is, as long as one lives in the world of reality, which we do, can there be the ending of suffering in that world of reality? Think about it. Look at it. Don't say yes, or no. If there is no ending of suffering in the world of reality—which brings order—if there is no ending of selfishness in the world of reality—it is selfishness that creates disorder in the world of reality—if there is no ending to that then you haven't understood, or grasped, the full significance of ending time. Therefore you have to bring about order in the world of reality, in the world of relationships, of action, of rational and irrational thinking, of fear and pleasure. So can one, living in the world of reality as we are, end selfishness? You know it is a very complex thing to end selfishness, it isn't just, "I won't think about myself". . . . This selfishness in the field of reality is creating chaos. And you are the world and the world is you. If you change deeply you affect the whole consciousness of man.

Chapter 15

THE UNIFYING FACTOR

WHAT IS THE unifying factor in meditation? Because that is one of the most necessary and urgent things. Politicians are not going to bring this unity however much they may talk about it. It has taken them thousands of years just to meet each other. What is that factor? We are talking about a totally different kind of energy, which is not the movement of thought with its own energy; and will that energy, which is not the energy of thought, bring about this unity? For God's sake, this is your problem, isn't it? Unity between you and your wife or husband, unity between you and another. You see, we have tried to bring about this unity; thought sees the necessity of unity and therefore has created a centre. As the sun is the centre of this world, holding all things in that light, so this centre created by thought hopes to bring mankind together. Great conquerors, great warriors, have tried to do this through bloodshed. Religions have tried to do it, and have brought about more division with their cruelty, with their wars, with their torture. Science has enquired into this. And because science is the accumulation of knowledge, and the movement of knowledge is thought, being fragmentary it cannot unify.

Is there an energy which will bring about this unity, this unification of mankind? We are saying, in meditation this energy comes about, because in meditation there is no centre. The centre is created by thought, but something else, totally different, takes place, which is compassion. That is the unifying factor of mankind. To be—not to become compassionate, that is again another deception—but to *be* compassionate.

That can only take place when there is no centre, the centre being that which has been created by thought—thought which hopes that by creating a centre it can bring about unity, like a fragmentary government, like a dictatorship, like autocracy, all those are centres hoping to create unity. All those have failed, and they will inevitably fail. There is only one factor, and that is this sense of great compassion. And that compassion *is* when we understand the full width and depth of suffering. That is why we talked a great deal about suffering, the suffering not only of a human being, but the collective suffering of mankind. Don't understand it verbally or intellectually but somewhere else, in your heart, feel the thing. And as you are the world and the world is you, if there is this birth of compassion you will inevitably bring about unity, you can't help it.